T0160233

CAN'T DO IT
YOURSELF

I had the profound privilege of working closely with Mike Leven for several years and have benefitted greatly from the depth of his wisdom. Now, in his eagerly anticipated book, Can't Do It Yourself, *a good deal of that wisdom is available to everyone, which is a rare gift.*

No matter one's title, profession, or level of success, there is only upside to reading Mike's book. It oozes authenticity and humility, just like Mike, and he shares valuable lessons learned throughout his career that all of us can apply. There is a reason Mike has received pretty much every lifetime achievement award given in the hospitality industry and why whenever anyone who knows him comes to town, they make it a point to stop by. Treasure this book—Mike is truly one of a kind and has my highest respect.

—Kenneth R. Greger, partner, August Leadership, LLC

What I like about Can't Do It Yourself *is that it provides seventy to eighty pithy life lessons. These lessons come from life experiences that shaped Mike's compassionate-based values and at the same time made him a fierce competitor. From front to back of CDIY are examples of Mike courageously taking bold risks by bringing together buddies, family, and/or teams to battle together over-whelming forces, prejudice, and misconceptions.*

—Philip C. Lee, founder,
Leaders Edge & Lead Together Mastery

I had the privilege of working for Mike. I claim him as my surrogate father in business. As he shares in his book, Mike leads through life lessons. Always wanting to be a teacher, he engages the people around him with humility, a caring and close relationship, and quickly giving the credit to others. He made complex strategies simple and always focused on taking care of the employees and customer. In these troubling times, Mike's approach to leadership and to life is refreshing, authentic, and rewarding.

—S. Kirk Kinsell, former CEO, IHG Americas

Talking the talk is easy. Mike Leven has spent his entire life walking the walk. The foundation of Mike's career, spanning over sixty years of extraordinary impact as a leader in business and philanthropy, is a personal, ethical, and moral compass that never wavers from true north. Mike Leven has inspired me for decades, and the life lessons he shares in Can't Do It Yourself *will be a beacon for anyone who reads this engrossing story of a life well lived.*

—James S. Grien, president & CEO, TM Capital

I have been associated with Mike Leven for over thirty-five years and have found him to be a great individual, probably the best in his field of hospitality. Mike has a keen mind and opinions that are studied and well thought out. Mike is a strategically forward thinker and his thoughts about our present situations and what the future looks like are serious and you should consider them to be prescient. He looks to the past to understand today and our future. This is true as a leader in the hospitality industry and the larger world around us. I trust Mike's judgement and I have followed his advice for years. This book is a must-read.

—Bernie Marcus, former CEO & cofounder, The Home Depot

Business bookshelves creak from the weight of immodest CEO hagiographies with soon-to-be-forgotten truisms. However, Mike Leven's reflections in Can't Do It Yourself *tower over the genre with his candid life and leadership retrospection. Leven is unusually humble and yet proud with durable messages for the ages. Leven's leadership model is different from the boastful titans of technology and other freewheeling individualists, which underplay the dependency upon others for a leader's success. In* Can't Do It Yourself, *Leven uniquely explains the way leaders must skillfully and responsibly leverage relationships across technologies, sectors, continents, communities, ages, gender, and races in vivid examples that bypass business clichés and Sunday School sermonizing. Leven's anchoring in principles is not PR-packaged image management clean-up after success but a self-aware way of life core to his success. A committed capitalist, Leven shows the path for doing good while doing well.*

—Jeffrey A. Sonnenfeld
  Senior Associate Dean for Leadership Studies,
  Lester Crown Professor of Leadership Practice,
  Yale School of Management

Can't Do It Yourself *represents living principles and values Mike believed and applied in his personal and professional life. The title of the book itself shows his broadness of mind, compassion, and humility of his heart.*

  This book is a true inspiration, full of real-life lessons Mike has recorded for those who want to use it as a guide and resource to navigate their own life as "compassionate leaders" for the betterment of humanity.

—H. P. Rama, chairman of the board, Auro Hotels

There is a problem with Can't Do It Yourself. *Once you start reading it, all other plans for the day are deferred. That is how compelling this book is.*

In addition to being relentlessly interesting, the book is relentlessly wise. That is because Mike Leven wrote it. And wisdom is the key to everything good in life—to happiness, to success, to making a good world.

Since very few schools—from elementary school to graduate school—teach wisdom, Mike Leven and his book are indispensable. If you are starting or developing a business, a high school or college student who wants to succeed in life, or just a human being wanting to understand life better—and be entertained by an amazing life story along the way—I cannot recommend Can't Do It Yourself *highly enough. It is a great book by a great man. Both are very rare.*

—Dennis Prager, nationally syndicated radio talk show host, president of the internet-based Prager University (PragerU), and *New York Times* bestselling author of ten books, including most recently volume two of *The Rational Bible*

CAN'T DO IT
YOURSELF

MIKE LEVEN

CAN'T DO IT
YOURSELF

*How Commitment to Others Leads
to Personal Prosperity*

Advantage.

Published by Advantage, Charleston, South Carolina.
Member of Advantage Media Group.

ADVANTAGE is a registered trademark, and the Advantage colophon is a trademark of Advantage Media Group, Inc.

Printed in the United States of America.

10 9 8 7 6 5 4 3 2

ISBN: 978-1-64225-162-3
LCCN: 2020912224

Cover design by Megan Elger.
Layout design by Wesley Strickland.

This publication is designed to provide accurate and authoritative information in regard to the subject matter covered. It is sold with the understanding that the publisher is not engaged in rendering legal, accounting, or other professional services. If legal advice or other expert assistance is required, the services of a competent professional person should be sought.

Advantage Media Group is proud to be a part of the Tree Neutral® program. Tree Neutral offsets the number of trees consumed in the production and printing of this book by taking proactive steps such as planting trees in direct proportion to the number of trees used to print books. To learn more about Tree Neutral, please visit **www.treeneutral.com**.

Advantage Media Group is a publisher of business, self-improvement, and professional development books and online learning. We help entrepreneurs, business leaders, and professionals share their Stories, Passion, and Knowledge to help others Learn & Grow. Do you have a manuscript or book idea that you would like us to consider for publishing? Please visit **advantagefamily.com** or call **1.866.775.1696**.

This book is dedicated to my wife, Andrea. For sixty years she has been my best friend, my adviser, my mentor, my psychiatrist, my teacher, my lover, and the mother and grandmother of my children and grandchildren. She is the one without whom the journey would never have been the same. I offer both my thanks and my apologies for the challenges she had to manage during our life together.

CONTENTS

ACKNOWLEDGMENTS xiii

INTRODUCTION 1

PART I 3

A STRONG FOUNDATION

CHAPTER 1 5

A CHILDHOOD IN BOSTON, 1937–1955

CHAPTER 2 23

RENAISSANCE MAN, 1955–1959

CHAPTER 3 37

TO WHOM IT MAY CONCERN, 1959–1961

PART II 49

EXPERIENCE AS EDUCATION

CHAPTER 4 51

SALES, 1961–1964

CHAPTER 5 67

OPERATIONS, 1965–1969

CHAPTER 6 83
COMMON VALUES, 1968–1971

CHAPTER 7 97
**A PASS, AN ELIMINATION, AND
AN ACHIEVEMENT, 1972–1974**

CHAPTER 8 113
THE SKY'S THE LIMIT, 1975–1985

PART III 125
THE DEFINITION OF SUCCESS

CHAPTER 9 127
EXPERIENCE AND PRINCIPLES, 1985–1989

CHAPTER 10 141
TOO OLD? 1989–2005

CHAPTER 11 159
RETIREMENT? 2005–2009

CHAPTER 12 169
LAS VEGAS SANDS, 2009–2014

CONCLUSION 189

APPENDIX 199

ACKNOWLEDGMENTS

I'd like to say thank you to the hundreds, or perhaps thousands, of people who have touched me and who I have touched over nearly eighty-three years of life. How fortunate it has been for me to know all of them: bosses, peers, employees, friends, family, and the ones most of you will never know about. The stories are too numerous for this book. But each human being has impacted me in ways that, as a young person, I could never have imagined. This work is perhaps a way of saying that, without you all, it could not have happened.

Lastly, I have to acknowledge Dana Kroos, the writer. From the original outline to the first interview to the last words, her patience, competence, and translation of my sentences were perfect. She made the writing easy and no problem. Also to Kristin Goodale and Nate Best, my administrator and editor, I thank them for their professional guidance and available assistance in completing the task at hand. They all proved that "can't do it yourself" is always the right way to go.

INTRODUCTION

"Why do you work so hard?" someone once asked me. The answer was twofold. First, I always felt a responsibility to do my job to the best of my ability, but also, I was sincerely interested in my work and in the people I encountered through my business endeavors. My understanding of business is not about numbers, hierarchies, and the bottom line; it is about the human side of business.

I worked for fifty-three years in the hospitality industry. Tourism brings people together. The hotel industry is comprised of places where different people come together for unique reasons. What I learned from this industry is that the values so near and dear to me are the same as those that are near and dear to others. Beyond being profitable, the hospitality industry can lead by example, showing tolerance by treating the many communities that we serve and employ with understanding.

My career was an education. I learned that at their cores, businesses are about people: the people whom they serve, the people whom they employ, and the people connected to the organizations with which the businesses collaborate. To be successful in business, you must understand the human side of decisions and interactions; you must form relationships and connect to people on a personal level.

It's been a long, hard, and wonderful road. I have learned so much. I am still learning. After fifty-three years, I can honestly say that I never compromised my ethics or values. I battled for the customers, for my employees, and for principled actions. What matters at the end of a long career is who you influenced and how you have influenced them. This is the story of what I learned during my career, how I came to learn those lessons, those who changed the course of my career and my life, and how my experience and knowledge helped me to influence others in positive ways.

> What matters at the end of a long career is who you influenced and how you have influenced them.

PART I

A STRONG
FOUNDATION

CHAPTER 1

A CHILDHOOD IN BOSTON, 1937–1955

THE APARTMENT IN MATTAPAN

Among the pictures in my condominium in Atlanta of my sons, my wife, my parents, the friends that I have made, and the places that I have been, there are two pictures of my maternal grandfather. One is a wedding photo taken in 1903 in which he and my grandmother stand stiffly in their wedding clothes, their tight expressions of concentration cast in fading sepia tones. He is so young that I often cannot really recognize him; he seems not to be another version of the man I knew but someone else entirely. Then sometimes I catch his image at the right angle, and I see the grandfather I knew in the near-smile on that young man's face. I want to tell him about the life that he will go on to lead, and about my life. I want to tell him all the ways that the decisions he is making then, and has already made, will guide not only the rest of his years but also mine.

The other photo that I have of my grandfather was taken in 1941 by an amateur photographer, my grandfather's youngest son, Lou. I am present in that photo, sitting on my grandfather's knee at four years old. I don't actually remember the moment, but I have built a memory around that image after looking at it for so many years. I can smell the starch of my grandfather's button-up shirt as well as the outdoors that soaked into his skin; I can feel the roughness and warmth of his hands around my arms. I know the sound of his laugh as it rose from his belly into his chest. Even then, I think he looked at me with great expectations.

My grandfather and grandmother lived with my parents and me until I was sixteen years old and then they moved to an old neighborhood in Roxbury, and we moved from the triplex to a duplex. I was raised in that intergenerational household with what was akin to two sets of parents. I am an only child, born in 1937 between the miscarriages of my less fortunate siblings, doted upon by both my parents and my grandparents. My mother, Sari, was a secretary who left her job when she was pregnant so that, along with my grandmother, Ida, she could stay home with me; my father, David, was a traveling salesman who was often away for many days at a time; and my grandfather, Frank Goldberg, was a foreman at the dungaree factory. Together we lived in the first-floor apartment of a triplex that my grandparents rented in Mattapan at 624 Norfolk Street, on the corner of Blue Hill Avenue. The apartment had three bedrooms, a boiler that had to be lit to procure hot water, a coal bin in the basement, and an ice box on the back porch where ice was delivered (since we had no refrigerator). We also had no air-conditioning and no washer or dryer. Although I was happy then, I did not truly understand the riches of that upbringing until I was older.

For the decades that my parents lived there, Mattapan was a unique community. Along with Dorchester and Roxbury, it comprised an area of Boston where over ninety thousand Jews lived in just three square miles. It was a safe and close-knit community filled with kosher butcher shops, delis (including the famous G&G Deli where presidential candidates frequently made stops to campaign), bakeries, eateries, cafés, movie theaters, synagogues, parks, the Young Men's Hebrew Association, bookstores, and schools. People shopped, ate, worked, learned, and played within those connected neighborhoods. As a child, I grew up coming home from school for a home-cooked lunch at noon, walking from Charles Logue Grammar School, to Hebrew school at Temple Beth Hillel every afternoon, and venturing out on my own after dinner and on weekends to find pickup games in the Norfolk Street Playground, to Boston on the trolley with friends, or to dances and part-time jobs as a teenager. On summer days, I would go out in the morning and not return home until dark. My parents never worried about me. It was the kind of community where people knew and took care of their neighbors, where fathers congregated on stair stoops on Sunday mornings and mothers spoke to one another while out running errands, where all the kids of roughly the same age ran together in friendly and gregarious packs, where grandparents told stories on park benches and young people listened. It was safe—we did not even have a key to lock our apartment—and mostly protected from the dangers, both criminal and social, of the outside world.

I had two especially good friends then, Norman Patz and Arnold Coran. The three of us grew close in our shared neighborhood, as casual play turned into formal clubs organized through schools and community centers. Together we were in Cub Scouts, the Jordan's of Mattapan, B'nai B'rith Youth AZA (Aleph Zadik Aleph), and the other formal groups where I had my first leadership experiences, becoming captain of the Jordan's football team and president of the AZA chapter. Eighty-three years later, I am still friends with both Norman, a retired rabbi, and Arnold, who became a famous pediatric surgeon at the

University of Michigan. It reminds me that even relationships that seem casual can be extremely significant. Many of the relationships and experiences from my youth came to have a great impact on my later life.

The neighborhood where I grew up was also a community of immigrants. Both of my parents were the children of immigrants, as was the case for most of my friends. These immigrants largely left their pasts behind. They did not teach their children their native languages or talk about the experiences that had pushed them to leave the countries where they were born. They embraced English and America, but they also kept with them the spirit of community and generosity that had helped them to survive in their past lives and to succeed in their transitions to Boston.

My grandfather was from a small town outside of Odessa, Slavita, Ukraine, in Crimea, Russia. He came to the US in 1896 when he was fifteen years old and met my grandmother, also an immigrant, from the farming town of Tavyan, Lithuania. They married in 1903 in the United States. Neither of them ever told me stories about the places where they were from. Although their first languages were Russian and Yiddish, they spoke only English to me. Even my mother did not speak Russian, and she understood only a rudimentary amount of Yiddish. Russian was a language that my grandparents left behind, and Yiddish was a language that they used on few occasions, together, when they needed to have a private conversation in the public space of our small apartment. I was always amazed when it made an appearance—a secret code between them.

My father often traveled when I was young. He sold paint for Lehman Brothers in New Jersey, working a territory from western Massachusetts to Rhode Island and Connecticut. He used to play catch with me on the small patch of grass on the side of our apartment.

He would often be home for a couple of days, then gone for a couple of days, home for a week, then gone the next week. When he was home, he would tell me about his customers. He spoke about them as though they were friends, recounting anecdotes about their kids, describing funny tricks that their dogs had been taught, and repeating jokes or stories that they told him. He often stayed in their homes overnight while on his trips, as though he was a relative who had come to town. His customers were important to him. He valued not only their business but also their respect and friendship. He knew how to take care of them.

My father also engaged me in the wider community of the city by taking me to sporting events. We saw Red Sox, Boston Braves, Boston Celtics, and Boston Patriots (as they were known then) games; the Boston Bruins play in the Stanley Cup playoffs; the 1948 World Series when the Boston Braves played Cleveland; and other major events that brought the entire city of Boston together. We saw "Hammerin' Hank" Greenberg play for the Pittsburgh Pirates against Boston. During batting practice, he threw a ball to me up in the stands. It went over my head, and I didn't catch it, but I fully appreciated his noticing me. In 1947, my father took me to Jackie Robinson's first game playing with the Brooklyn Dodgers against the Boston Braves at the Braves field in Boston. When he took the field, the crowd in the stands behind us shouted derogatory remarks, calling him names and telling him to go home. He looked confident as he jogged out onto the field, engaged fully in the goal at hand. But I was bothered by the harassment from the fans. I was ten years old, and both his appearance and the reception he was given had a major effect on me.

In 1943, my father was drafted into World War II and was gone for two years, eventually fighting in the Battle of the Bulge, Seventh Armored Division of Patton's Third Army. I had nine relatives who fought in World War II; one did not survive. One of my relatives, a cousin named Chester Gelbert, came to live with us after he was discharged so that he could attend Northeastern University. Chester was my grandfather's oldest son's son. He became like an older brother to me during those four years that he stayed in our guest room before he left to take a job working for DuPont in Delaware. I asked my grandfather once why his last name was Goldberg, and Chester's last name (and the names of my uncles Barney and Lou) was Gelbert. He explained that the younger generation had changed their names so that they would not be discriminated against and could get jobs.

My father sent letters during the years that he was away at war, and I imagine that it was a very tense time for my mother, although she never showed her worry. For me it was like my father was on an extended work trip. In his absence, I still had three adults to care for me.

My father returned home before Christmas in 1945. A few months later, he borrowed a 1946 Chevrolet, one of the first cars off the line, from my uncle, and we drove with my father's mother—an immigrant from Lithuania who also lived near Boston—to Miami for a vacation. It took us five and a half days to make the drive, and another five and a half days to drive back, all for a weeklong stay in Florida. The trip was as much about the drive from the East Coast to the South and back as it was about our days relaxing on the beach. It was my first real experience outside of our Boston neighborhood.

I remember the sign that announced we had crossed the Mason-Dixon Line when we left Pennsylvania. We drove on to Richmond, Virginia, and stopped for lunch. There, for the first time in my life, I saw water fountains and bathrooms labeled "white" and "colored."

"What does that mean?" I asked my parents.

I can't recall exactly how they explained segregation to me, only that they recognized that it was an odd and unfair concept.

Our trip through the southern states continued to reveal things that were foreign and ugly to me. We traveled on old roads, Routes 301 and 17, lined with dilapidated shacks where the descendants of slaves lived. Children my age played outside in ragged clothes, barefoot, with punctured and flat basketballs, or with baseballs that had lost their leather, using sticks in place of bats. There was something strange as well as something familiar about it.

In Miami, we stayed at a kosher hotel called the Lord Balfour (my grandmother was kosher). I know now that the hotel was named for Lord Balfour who wrote the Balfour Declaration, which became a large part of the Zionist movement. The hotel is still there, although now it is a boutique hotel.

During the next week, as we went to cafés, beaches, restaurants, and parks, I read signs that said, "No Negroes. No Jews. No dogs."

"Why do they have those signs?" I asked my parents. At nine years old, I wasn't bothered, but I was curious.

"It's just like that in the South," my parents told me.

When I was older, we went to Cape Cod in the summers—after Labor Day when the rates were lower. I saw that same sign in the windows of restricted hotels: "No Negroes. No Jews. No dogs." That kind of discrimination had been normalized and was largely invisible. In 1947, the Academy Award-winning film *Gentleman's Agreement* was released starring Gregory Peck as a journalist posing as a Jew to uncover the discrimination of Jews in resort hotels. It gave context and shape to what I had seen a few years earlier. Those types of institutional restrictions lasted until the 1960s when, as a young salesman, I was representing hotels that had policies against taking Jews. Informally, such restrictions lasted even longer. In 1981, when moving my family to the suburbs north of Chicago, my real estate broker informed me that I could not buy a house in a town called Kenilworth because I was a Jew.

HOMELAND

From a young age, I was involved in many activities, and I loved sports and theater. My only burden was Hebrew school, which demanded a great deal of my time, taking place Monday, through Thursday and Sunday mornings for two hours at a time. I had to squeeze it in after school before sports started from the age of seven until thirteen. I received good marks in Hebrew school, but I always got a C in conduct because I didn't behave very well; it was difficult for me not to resent the time it took away from my play.

I played baseball in pickup games in my neighborhood at the Almont Street and Norfolk Playgrounds nearly every day. Sports and theater created level playing fields that were color blind and transcended the prejudices of workplaces and neighborhood divisions. It was a space removed from social and political pressures, where those involved were immersed solely in the game or the show. Although a lot of the boys I played baseball with were Jewish, they were also Irish Catholic and Greek as well as anyone of around the same age who had a mitt and a passion for the game. We gathered on sunny afternoons in a sandlot, split ourselves into teams, and played for hours, sometimes arguing over pitches and tags but mostly just loving the game.

When I was twelve, I was playing baseball at the Almont Street Playground that was near Saint Angela's Church. I was a pretty good baseball player, and I was precocious at that time, taking a lead in solving conflicts and cheering on my teammates. That day there was a priest named Father O'Leary watching the game. When the game was over, Father O'Leary came to me and said, "You're a pretty good baseball player. Would you like to play in the CYO League?"

I knew that he was referring to the Catholic Youth Organization. There was no Little League baseball at that time; instead, teams and games were often organized through religious and community organizations.

I said, "Sure, Father. I'd be happy to play."

"What's your name?" he asked.

"Michael Leven," I told him.

He flinched, then nodded. With a sigh, he said, "Sorry, you can't play."

That was the first experience that I can recall of being directly discriminated against. Although it was relatively innocuous, it was a glimpse of how the larger world perceived me beyond the safety of my small community.

At home I listened to Red Sox games on the radio and played pinochle with my grandfather, talked to my mother and grandmother while they cooked together in the kitchen, and tossed the ball in the side yard with my father, who interrupted our games occasionally to wave to neighbors or start brief conversations.

On some evenings, my grandparents would invite relatives and friends from the old country over for tea or to play bingo for pennies. They would sit at the dining room table laughing and debating, talking about the price of meat, or the change in weather, or the ways that children were growing up and others were growing old all around them. My grandfather always had good friends. He was the vice president of a modern Orthodox synagogue where we went on Saturdays and holidays. I fondly remember carrying my grandmother's prayer book to the synagogue on high holidays when she was not allowed to carry anything heavy.

My grandfather never made much money at the dungaree factory, but that didn't seem to bother him. I remember friends and neighbors coming to see him when they had problems. With what little money my grandfather had, he was always engaged in philanthropy. He willingly loaned money to friends in need, who were often never able to pay him back, or donated to causes in the neighborhood. At times he borrowed money himself so that he could give to others. Every Friday, a bearded old man came to the back door of our apartment to exchange a blue box from the Jewish National Fund that my grandfather would fill with pennies during the week.

My grandfather woke at five o'clock every morning. Often, I would get up and sit at the table with him while he drank his tea. He would talk to me about school and baseball. Sometimes we would listen to the radio. He listened to the radio often as a way of improving his English pronunciation, concentrating on each word. He loved the Lone Ranger.

The only time I saw my grandfather cry, he was listening to the radio. I came home one Saturday afternoon and sat with him as he listened. It was 1947. I was ten years old. He was bent over the table holding a pencil to a piece of paper, listening intently to the broadcast and writing down numbers. I had never seen him write on the Sabbath. I had no idea what was happening. His eyes were red-rimmed, then tears streaked his face and dripped onto the paper, soaking the marks that he had made. He continued to listen and to write.

"Why are you crying?" I asked.

"We have a home," he said.

He was listening to a broadcast from the United Nations where the general assembly was voting on a resolution to partition Palestine and create the Jewish State of Israel—a vote intentionally taken on the Jewish Sabbath to hinder the Israeli case. On the paper, he was tallying and counting the votes as they were reported. "We have a home," he repeated.

That moment stuck with me. When I was older and I thought of it with a broader perspective, I saw my grandfather as a smart man who had never gone to college, who had come to the US when he was fifteen years old and speaking no English. He never hoped to accomplish anything financially in his lifetime; he wanted only a manageable life for himself and a better life for his children. He received that communal homeland, granted by a political power to which he had no real connection, as a personal gift. He had been recognized. He had been given a place.

His emotional response had a major effect on me. I knew about, but cared little for, the State of Israel before that (and maybe even in the years after), but I was touched by how dear it was to him. My grandfather never got to Israel. In 1971, I had a business assignment there and I took my father, who had also never been, with me. It was a major event in his life. To this day, I still do a great deal of work and make contributions to Israel. It is important to me, but equally important to me is how much it meant to my grandfather. This commitment was far more important to him than any of my other successes.

A FORMAL EDUCATION

In the Boston public school system, you had to make a choice about which high school to attend. You either went to your assigned neighborhood school or applied for one of the magnet programs that offered more specialized instruction. In ninth grade, I started at the all-boys Boston Latin School and graduated in 1955. Founded in 1635, Boston Latin School is the oldest public high school in the US. It offers a rigorous program focused on classical and traditional studies. When I attended Boston Latin School, my entering class was six hundred students, and by graduation, that same class had been cut in half as students dropped out or failed. My experiences there entirely changed my relationship to academics. The school was disciplined and demanded academic dedication. It transformed the way I studied. I graduated sixty-two in the class, which was a very high ranking at the time. Nearly one hundred of the three hundred graduates that year went to Harvard.

Boston Latin School also offered competitive organized sports. When I missed the baseball team tryouts, I turned to basketball. I had played a lot of basketball with the Young Men's Hebrew Association in Roxbury. I made the junior varsity team as a freshman. My senior year, in 1955, our team won the city championship.

The rigor and opportunities provided by Boston Latin School helped to shape and nurture my interests and talents as a young man. As an adult, I remain involved in the school and have worked to both show my gratitude and ensure that the school can continue to offer positive and life-changing experiences for students. In 2017, I cochaired a capital campaign that raised $54 million for the school. For my philanthropic efforts, the school granted me an award and honored me in the Founders Gallery, where my name appears with other accomplished alumni and supporters of the school. It is an honor of which I am very proud.

While I had many successes at Boston Latin School, I had some disappointments. We did a lot of SAT preparation at Boston Latin, and although I committed myself to studying, I did poorly on the SAT. The college counselor asked me to take the exams again—they seemed to be the one thing holding me back from an exceptional college application. I did a little better the second time around, and the counselor said, "I think that I can get you into Harvard," but he didn't seem certain, and I didn't want to compete with my peers who had better academics. I decided instead to go to Tufts. Then, during my senior year, I ran for vice president of my class and lost the election to a young man named John Dobbyn. John Dobbyn was Irish, the young man who won the presidency, David Rosenthal, was Jewish, and the young man who won secretary was Bob Watkins, one of only two African American students in the class.

From ages ten until sixteen, my parents also sent me to Camp Tevya in New Hampshire for eight weeks every summer. It was, in many ways, a typical Jewish summer camp. Located on the shore of a lake, it was comprised of sleeping cabins, a kosher dining hall, community centers, gyms, tennis courts, outdoor fields, and a theater. The camp offered activities ranging from religious services to athletics and arts. Camp Tevya was where I was really exposed to acting. I became very involved in the theater program and worked and acted in several shows.

When I graduated from the camp at sixteen years old, I approached the camp director, Aaron Gordon, who was also a teacher at Boston Latin, and told him that I wanted to return the following year as a counselor.

He looked me in the eye and said, "You're not mature enough to be a counselor."

I was crushed. Those experiences—losing the election at Boston Latin, getting a poor score on the SAT, and being turned down for a position at Camp Tevya—were the first real encounters that I had with failure and outright rejection. Many things came easily for me—athletics, theater, academics—and I couldn't yet embrace the struggle and defeat that is necessary for growth.

The following summer I started the first of several summer jobs that I would have through the rest of high school and into college. I had my first job the first summer after I graduated from Camp Tevya, in 1953, when I was sixteen, as a soda jerk in a drugstore around the corner from our apartment in Mattapan. It paid only forty-two and a half cents an hour, but I got free milkshakes, and I also got experience working with customers.

Then I started my own lawn mowing business. I mowed lawns for a dollar an hour with a push mower that I borrowed from my uncle. Eventually I became too sick to do the work and went to the doctor. There was a polio epidemic that year, and in general, people were on edge. My illness, however, was work related: I was having serious leg problems from the physical labor. I had to quit about three quarters of the way through the summer.

During the summer of 1954, I was hired as a kitchen boy at Camp Avoda in Middleborough, Massachusetts, where I made twenty-five dollars for eight weeks and got free room and board. I was happy to be back in a summer camp community where I had lots of opportunities to play basketball and softball. The following summer, in 1955, after I graduated from high school, Camp Avoda hired me as a counselor. In that role I learned about working with a range of people: I had to manage the kids, communicate with the parents when they came, and work with other counselors and my boss. Because we were all living together, it was an intense and accelerated education. I never realized that it was going to help me understand management and succeed in business later on.

The next year, after my first year of college, the director of Camp Tevya called and said, "You can come back now. You've grown up, and I would like to hire you as a junior counselor."

I went back to a camp that I loved and continued to work and develop skills in communicating, leading, organizing, and engaging in community projects. Eventually I became athletic director and assistant head counselor and also played many roles in the annual counselor shows, including Henry Higgins in *My Fair Lady*, Harold Hill in *The Music Man*, Nicely-Nicely Johnson in *Guys and Dolls*, and the manager in *Damn Yankees*.

"BE A GOOD LAWYER"

My grandfather died in 1956. By then, my mother, father, and I had moved to an apartment at 26 Egmont Street in Brookline, where many of the Jewish people moved when leaving the Dorchester/Mattapan/Roxbury section of Boston. By 1968, almost all the Jewish residents had moved away from the Dorchester/Mattapan/Roxbury area. When my grandfather had a stroke and was admitted to Beth Israel Hospital, I was nineteen, a freshman in college, and living at home.

We spoke for a while when I went to visit him. He wanted me to be a lawyer. I had been talking to him for a while about going to law school, which, at the time, seemed like what I wanted to do. In eighth grade, in preparation for high school, one of my teachers had assigned an exploration into a possible career. Students had written papers about people they admired and their professional achievements. I wrote about Samuel Leibowitz, the famous Romanian-born defense attorney who defended the Scottsboro Boys, a group of African American youths falsely accused of rape and sentenced to death in 1931. I was distraught by the obvious injustice perpetrated on the young men, who were around my age, and also impressed by Leibowitz's integrity and courage as well as the ability of one man to have such a major effect on the lives of others. I wanted to be like Samuel Leibowitz. I used to come home and tell my grandfather, "I'm going to be a lawyer."

The last words that my grandfather spoke to me were, "Be a good lawyer." I had been like a son to him all those years, and he had been like a second father to me. I did not become a lawyer. But what I hear now when I remember those words is, "Be good. Do good. Go out into the world and become the person who you want to be."

I often ask myself, "Why do I do what I do? Why am I like this? Why do some things bother me and others do not bother me?" All these parts of my personality—the decisions that I make, the opportunities that I seize, the prospects that I seek out—are based on a foundation that was taking shape in my childhood.

As a child, I was exposed to many different kinds of people as well as to varied experiences. While my father and grandfather engaged me in sports, it was important to my mother that I learn to appreciate the arts. From a very young age, she began to expose me to music, theater, and museums. She used to take me on the trolley to the Boston Symphony. I remember the exhilaration of seeing "Peter and the Wolf," the music playing out the emotions of the animals, the audience aware of the danger through the tenor tones of the oboe long before the duck knew to be afraid. In grammar school, my mother signed me up for tap dancing lessons, which I disliked, but attended. In college, when I was acting in plays, I would rehearse my lines in the kitchen for my grandmother, who had moved in with us after my grandfather died, and my mother, who would look up over steaming pots and ironing boards and applaud when I was done. I did not become a symphony musician, or a dancer, or a professional actor. These influences were not so direct. And yet these experiences, like the other experiences of my life—the community that I grew up in, the history that I was exposed to, the people who I came to know—formed who I am.

Lessons Learned

1. Family is important, but it is also important to be a part of a larger community of people.

2. Lifelong friends can be yours from the beginning. Keep them.

3. Success, as shown by my father's business, comes from the customers.

4. Segregation and discrimination have proven themselves to be negative practices and to be detrimental to humanity.

5. No matter your economic status, be generous and give whatever you can to others.

6. Natural skills will take a person only so far. Hard work is the key to achieving a better outcome.

7. Your childhood—good or bad—is just part of your foundation, not an end in itself.

CHAPTER 2

RENAISSANCE MAN, 1955–1959

COMMUTER

As a child, I stayed close to my family and neighborhood. It was in college that I stepped out on my own and eventually sought to find and build my own community. In doing this, I learned a great deal about other people, and I also came to better understand my own apprehensions and goals. I defined what I would embrace and what I would discard. I firmly established my personal limits and the boundaries of my tolerance, solidifying the ethics that I would carry with me into my professional life.

My first semester at Tufts was socially challenging. I loved my courses, which offered a view of the world beyond my insular childhood. I took political science, theater, art history, and psychology. I also took classes in Bible studies and comparative religions because I wanted to understand the beliefs of others. One of my assignments was to attend different church services each week, moving from orthodox to liberal religions. The experience opened my eyes to the different ways that people practiced their faiths, and many years later, it provided practical knowledge when I found myself working with a man who explained that his behavior was dictated by his Presbyterian faith, something about which I had learned a great deal. I also took a speech course, taught by a Harvard law student, where students were asked to make a political speech. I made an argument that, although China's government was different from the governments of many Western nations, China had a right to be admitted to the United Nations—an unpopular notion at the time. Overall, the mixture of courses that I took represented my curious nature and my desire to understand how other people thought. They exposed me to new perspectives and gave me a foundation to handle interpersonal relationships.

My best friends from high school had all gone to Harvard. At Tufts, I was very much alone. My sense of estrangement was exacerbated by my status as a commuter that first semester. I attended courses as though going to work, driving to school each morning and returning home to my parents' house in the evenings. Other than my participation on the freshman basketball team, I had little involvement in the school. I was disconnected from my peers at Tufts.

It was really by chance that I joined a fraternity. No one in my purview—in my family or among my friends—was ever in a fraternity, and I knew very little about them. During rush week at the end of the first semester, I wandered into a party at the Alpha Epsilon Pi fraternity—one of only two fraternities on campus that accepted Jewish students. I didn't know anyone there, and no one knew me, but something about the community was immediately appealing. I talked for a while with a fraternity brother named Dick Werby. When it came time to select inductees, Dick strongly promoted me. I got a bid.

Becoming part of the fraternity completely changed my experience at Tufts. In the instant I joined, I belonged somewhere. Although it was a financial stretch for my parents, they found a way to support my move to campus the following semester. Once an only child, I became a brother in the fraternity.

For the rest of the time that I was at Tufts, I ate, studied, and socialized with my fraternity brothers. We played intramural sports together—I made the fraternity all-star teams in football and basketball. There was a sense of camaraderie that, before then, I had experienced only with my family.

In October 2019, I went to San Diego, where Dick Werby lives now, to give a speech. I met Dick for lunch. "I just wanted to tell you," I said to Dick, "that if it weren't for you, my life would be very different." If I hadn't joined the fraternity, I may not have stayed at Tufts after that lonely first semester, made the lifelong connections I made there, or had the experiences that did so much to shape my character and understanding of what it meant to be a part of a community and lead others.

With a shrug, Dick Werby said that he just thought that I would be a good fraternity brother. "When I asked the fraternity brothers to give you a bid, it was just because I liked you," he said. "I never would've expected that you'd have a career like you've had."

It's amazing how one small act can influence another person's life so profoundly. I continued to keep that in mind during the decades that followed when I was in business and making decisions that I knew could significantly affect the people around me.

MAYORAL CANDIDATESHIP

My membership in the Alpha Epsilon Pi fraternity not only spurred my complete involvement in Tufts but also led to both remarkable and challenging leadership opportunities. My fraternity class was exceptional. We built an excellent reputation on campus—number one in academic achievement as well as first place in multiple athletic championships, including the football championship, which was a rare win for a Jewish fraternity at that time. I was proud of what we were doing. In the following years, I played on the varsity lacrosse team and acted in school theater productions. I was also a sports editor and writer for the newspaper, a radio broadcaster for basketball games and football games, and eventually ran for the position of mayor of Tufts, a figurehead position. My orientation to college went from outside observation my first semester to leading the way by the next year.

During my sophomore year, the Alpha Epsilon Pi fraternity nominated me to run in the mayoral race at Tufts the following year. It was a big commitment that required a great deal of preparation, including garnering support from different clubs and factions of the campus. I got involved with the theater at Tufts to broaden my base of support and to practice for the candidateship, which was more an act of entertainment than a political run.

I began by volunteering in the theater and taking courses in the theater department as a sophomore. By the next year, I was playing roles in shows, including *The Crucible, The Wizard of Oz*, and multiple Shakespeare productions. The theater was diverse and tolerant in a way that the rest of the campus was not, and I felt very comfortable there. I used the experience that I'd gained at Camp Tevya as a camper and then as a counselor.

During my senior year, I organized, produced, and directed the play *Stalag 17*, which was presented to the entire campus, casting my fraternity brothers in the roles. We rented an auditorium, trained someone on lighting, put on our own makeup, made costumes—the works. It resulted in a three-night performance presented as a gift to the school from the fraternity. It was an incredible experience and undertaking.

But before that show, I put my talents to the test in the Tufts mayoral candidateship. There was one other contender. As part of the race, each candidate chose a persona. *Maverick* was on TV then, and I chose Diamond Mike, the Mississippi riverboat gambler. My competitor was Huckleberry Finn. One of the assigned events was to put on a musical.

My fraternity organized a phenomenal campaign that was far superior to our competitor's. It was shocking when we lost. Although I took the loss well, I used to ask people what happened. No one had a definite answer. My guess is that Huck won by a very narrow margin.

Tufts ended the mayoral campaigns after that year, deciding that it took attention away from academics. I never again saw the man who ran as Huckleberry Finn. I have continued to perform songs from our original show at class reunions, most recently the fiftieth and fifty-fifth. Although my fraternity lost, it is our campaign run that the school remembers. It really goes to show that winning isn't everything, or that the official declaration of a winner doesn't always recognize the true champion of a contest.

Some people believed, although I have no evidence of this fact, that I did not win the mayoral race because I was seen on campus before the vote going out with an African American woman. I didn't date at all in high school and was inexperienced when I started dating in college—experience is so important. Before the actual campaign, I met a young actress named Terry Williams while I was working at the theater checking coats. *A Member of the Wedding* was playing, and Terry was in the production. There was a Louis Armstrong concert coming to campus. I wanted to go, but I didn't have a date. "By the way," I said to her one evening, "you going to the Louis Armstrong concert?"

"Not yet," she said.

"You want to come with me?" I asked. I didn't really think of it as a date, and I don't think that she did either.

I picked her up in front of her dorm, and we arrived at the concert about fifteen minutes late. It was dark when we walked in, and we were hit by the spotlights from the stage. Terry was in a gorgeous orange dress, and at that point, I was already growing long sideburns so that I could play the role of Diamond Mike. The place was silent, and for a moment, we were the center of everyone's attention.

I didn't think anything of it at the time—we sat down and enjoyed the concert—but the next day people on campus were talking about us. It was a major deal. The general consensus when I lost the mayoral race was that I'd lost because people opposed my interracial dating. I have no evidence that this is true. I think it's as likely that everyone was looking for a reason for why I lost, but it did highlight that there were people who thought differently than I—things that were of no concern to me were a dramatic disturbance for others.

Some years later, the woman who directed my mayoral campaign, Elaine Kasparian, told me that she thought Terry had a crush on me.

"Why didn't you tell me? Nobody told me," I said. I was truly naive about women and dating at that time.

I lost track of Terry after school. Then many years later, I saw her picture in a magazine. I hadn't spoken to her for twenty-five or thirty years, and I decided to call her. She was working with the schools in the Bronx and doing well.

PRESIDENT AND TOUGH DECISIONS

I gradually moved upward through positions in Alpha Epsilon Pi until, as a senior, I was elected president of the fraternity, a promotion that was both an honor and a responsibility. When I'd entered the fraternity, it did not have a good reputation on campus, but by the time my class graduated, we had earned the respect of the university. So much depended on reputation. We had worked hard, moving into the lead roles in various departments, becoming editors of the newspaper, being accepted to top graduate schools, and achieving other awards that reflected well on the university. Because we were held in high regard, we were given more opportunities on campus and beyond. During my tenure as president, I worked diligently to build and maintain this reputation. This meant that I had to make several difficult decisions that forced me to examine my priorities as a leader and community member. One concerned the fraternity's chef, an older man retired from the navy. He was an incredible cook.

The chef lived in Boston, about a mile from my parents' apartment, just over the Boston line from Brookline on Beacon Street, near Fenway Park. I often went home on Friday evenings to have dinner with my family. One Friday, when the chef saw me heading out, he asked if I could give him a ride home. It was the fall of 1959.

When I dropped him at his apartment, he invited me in for a beer. We chatted a little about the weather, Tufts, and the fraternity. Then there was a turn in the conversation. It took me a moment to realize what was happening: he was soliciting me. Then he became more direct.

"Excuse me," I said, remaining polite. "I don't want to participate in what you're talking about." I started to leave but then added, "Look, you can be who you are. It's not a problem for me, but don't touch my fraternity brothers." I was shielding my friends, who might be put in the same uncomfortable position, but moreover, I was feeling protective of the reputation of the fraternity as a whole. This is the kind of thing that no one has to worry about in 2020, but in 1959, rumors about homosexual relationships within the house could have ruined the fraternity. I didn't want anyone to get hurt, but at the same time, I didn't want to demonize the chef. I was walking a thin and fragile line. I didn't say to him, "You can't be a homosexual" or "I don't approve of your homosexuality." Instead, I put a restriction on his behavior: "Don't involve the fraternity." I had tolerance for his individual difference but could not tolerate any behavior that would jeopardize the fraternity.

The chef seemed to understand, and for a while, things carried on as before. The chef continued to come to work and to cook our meals.

Breakfast was served every morning à la carte. Brothers would arrive to the dining hall and help themselves to what was set out or order omelets from the chef. It was very casual. Brothers arrived wearing the boxers and T-shirts they had slept in. I noticed that the chef was watching them in a peculiar way—he had likely been watching us this way all along, but I hadn't realized it. I didn't say anything. I figured that things had been fine this long, and they would continue to be fine. Unfortunately, that wasn't the case.

The chef had a bedroom on the first floor, just off the kitchen, at the bottom of the stairs. He would often take a nap there in the afternoon or stay a night during the week. One afternoon I went downstairs to the kitchen for a glass of milk, and the door to the chef's bedroom was slightly ajar. I could see that the chef was involving himself with one of the fraternity brothers in his room. I didn't say anything to them then, but at the next fraternity meeting, I made a motion to fire the chef.

At the weekly meeting, I explained the situation to my lieutenant master, who seconded the motion. Then the discussion was opened to the floor, and I told my fraternity brothers about the situation. I was careful not to identify the brother who I had seen with the chef. "Our reputation is at stake," I told them. And it was. It was 1959, and the world would not have been tolerant of a homosexual relationship between the chef and a fraternity brother. I had worked for years to build that reputation, but I understood the fragility of the perceptions the community had of our fraternity. A rumor about the chef could have instantly damaged our standing. "I think that we have to let the guy go," I told my brothers.

My fraternity brothers seemed to agree with me, but they did not want to fire the chef; they liked his cooking. A few brothers stood and said, "I don't care what the guy did. I like his food."

I argued.

We took it to a vote and I lost.

"Fine," I said. "If you're not going to vote to dismiss the chef, I quit." I gave the gavel to the lieutenant master and left.

I sat alone in the library for about ten minutes before two of my brothers came upstairs and said to me, "We took another vote. You can fire him."

We got a new chef shortly thereafter. His food was terrible. Every day for the next five months until I graduated, my fraternity brothers busted my backside about how lousy the food was. But I never questioned my decision.

Sometimes people ask me where I learned to be a manager. My education came from a series of large and small experiences. Managing people is often about making difficult decisions, and you often don't know at the time whether you are making the correct decision. You try to do the right thing—the thing that is best for the community, or for the future, or for the most people. You set parameters and rely on a set of values to guide you. You can't know what the result will be until it happens and then you make another decision.

It is important to understand that institutions are temporary; they are run by people who come and go—a constantly changing dynamic. People have the capacity to build success, and people have

CAN'T DO IT YOURSELF

the capacity to tear that success down. Years later I would look back on many accomplishments only to see some of those mitigated or reversed by those that came after. As a young man, I learned at Camp Tevya from my boss and mentor, Aaron Gordon, that leadership sets standards and models the values for the institution. He was careful who he hired. He employed students from Boston Latin and other young people who he had known as campers and made them wait and grow into mature young adults who were ready to do the job before he employed them. He knew that you have to have good bones—good employees or people. He also knew that to have a good camp, or company, or club, or fraternity, you have to manage those people and direct them to work together in a cohesive and constructive way that supports an overall goal or philosophy.

As a young man, I had already learned a lot about leadership, although I had not thought about it directly. I made a choice that semester to put the reputation of the fraternity—something on which the current, future, and past brothers depended—above the welfare of one individual (or tasty food). It was a difficult decision. It was the first time that I had to terminate anyone. When I fired the chef, he left quietly, as though he was expecting it or as though such things had happened before. When I see my old fraternity brothers now, we sometimes still talk about that decision. The world has changed a great deal since then. Today my concerns would be very different.

HOW I MET MY WIFE

I met the head of the Modern Dance Club, Betty Bao, during the mayoral campaign. I had to dance in a musical production that was part of the campaign, and I had never danced on stage before. Betty gave me dance lessons to help me prepare.

Betty was Taiwanese American. Her father was a part of the Taiwanese delegation at the UN, and Betty was very well educated, kind, and wonderful. After I lost the vote, we started dating. We were both well known on campus: I was the president of my fraternity and very involved with the university; Betty was head cheerleader, gregarious, and participated in a lot of activities.

I was playing lacrosse then, and Betty came to a game. My dad was also there—he came to many of my games—and I was anxious for him to meet her. "Did you see her?" I asked after the game. She had been wearing a Chinese-style dress and stood out in the crowd.

"Yes," was all he said.

In the locker room after the game, I told my dad, "I think I'm going to marry that girl."

My dad didn't answer. He stood and walked out of the locker room.

At home, I mentioned my dad's response to my mother, and she said, "Don't worry, it'll pass."

One of my fraternity brothers named Henry White was also concerned about my relationship with Betty. He didn't know her really, only that she was both of a different race and of a different faith than I. My parents knew Henry's parents, who lived in New York City in their neighborhood, and the family connection likely heightened Henry's concern. He and Chickie, his girlfriend at the time and who later became his wife, sought a solution. They set me up on a date with Chickie's roommate, Andrea. I was still going out with Betty. Andrea went to Boston University and was also in a relationship with a young man at Dartmouth, so a relationship between us didn't seem likely. I met Andrea in January 1959, after she came home tan from winter break in Florida. She was a very New York type. I wasn't particularly interested, and she wasn't interested in me either. That's how I met my future wife.

Later, in May of that year, during the fraternity production of *Stalag 17*, Henry and Chickie brought Andrea to the play. I met her again. Betty and I had broken up by then, and Andrea had broken up with the student at Dartmouth. Andrea looked a little different to me at the second meeting, or I thought about her differently.

After I graduated from Tufts, I was heading to law school in Chicago. Henry and Chickie were engaged by this time. Days before I went away, I went for coffee with Chickie and her two roommates, one of whom was Andrea. My dad also came along. When we returned home, my dad said to me, "Did you see Andrea?"

"Sure," I said. "She was sitting right there."

"I like her a lot," he said. "I think that you should ask her out the next time you're home." I was busy then and distracted. I might not have noticed her had my father not pointed me in that direction. His comment planted a seed in my mind.

Andrea and I began corresponding long distance and eventually started dating.

While I can recall big decisions that I know changed the direction of my life or the lives of others, I am aware that often it is the small interactions—talking to someone at a party, taking a woman to a concert, meeting a woman for coffee—that end up changing our lives in the most significant ways. These small interactions have the power to redirect us or to teach us the lessons that we carry with us forever.

I saw Betty again at my twenty-fifth reunion. She had married a different Caucasian guy named Winston Lord III, who was part of the Pillsbury family and became ambassador to China. She wrote two books, had a couple of kids, and seemed to be doing really well. She looked at me and said, "Gee, you lost your hair." She married very well and so did I.

Lessons Learned

8. Loneliness is detrimental to a person. People need to be a part of something larger than themselves.

9. A single person or a single discussion can have a substantial impact on your life.

10. Managing others to a successful result is more satisfying than doing something only for yourself.

11. When disappointed by a loss, move on quickly.

12. Making a decision, especially about people, is very hard in the moment, but for the best results, you need to look at the bigger picture.

13. Leadership makes a significant difference to the performance of those being led.

14. Parenting is management; parents influence the decisions of their children.

15. Don't be afraid to ask questions about what you can do better. Admit when you don't know or when you make a mistake.

CHAPTER 3

TO WHOM IT MAY CONCERN, 1959–1961

LAW SCHOOL

My graduate education was marked by letters written to, from, and about me—typed and handwritten, words that were carefully placed and set in ink on paper. There is something precious about this sort of communication that takes a physical form—a thing that can be wrapped in an envelope, held, and kept. Those letters revealed the personalities of their writers both through language and through the swirled slants of their signatures. They expressed the relationships that I had and tracked the developments of those relationships in a concrete record. I still have many of them.

After I graduated from Tufts, I thought that I would become a lawyer. I scored very well on the LSAT but not well enough to get into Harvard or Yale. Instead, I applied to the five next best law schools: Stanford, University of Michigan, University of Chicago, New York University, and Columbia.

I thought that I would go to Columbia. The father of one of my very good friends was a partner in a law firm in New York. My friend was hoping to go to Columbia. He said that if we both got in, we could be roommates. It also seemed like I might be given a job at his father's firm after law school. My future seemed set.

I was accepted to every one of the five law schools to which I applied. Then Tufts offered me the one annual full-tuition scholarship they awarded each year for a student to go to the University of Chicago. I was still set on going to Columbia, but when my friend's application was rejected, my plan fell apart. I decided to take the scholarship and go to the University of Chicago.

I was the pride of my mother and father's eyes. No one in either of their families had ever been to law school. I was the first person in the Leven family to actually graduate from college and one of only a select few in the Goldberg family—my mother's family—to finish college.

Graduate school was a major move for other reasons as well. My journey to Chicago marked the first real time—other than summers at Camp Tevya—that I was away from home. My roommate was a fellow student from Tufts named Richard Bogosian, who later became a foreign service officer and an ambassador, but other than Richard, I knew no one. There were about 120 people in my class—only one woman and no people of color. I was lonely there. It was a very tough environment. The professors were critical and confrontational in class. It was a good law school, and I learned a lot in my first trimester, but it wasn't the friendliest place. I threw myself into my studies. I worked hard and tried to do well.

Andrea and I wrote letters back and forth that first trimester that I was away—neither of us could afford phone calls. She told me about her studies in education at Boston University. I told her about law school and Chicago. When I wrote to Henry about coming home for the break, he wrote back asking if I wanted to go out with him and Chickie on New Year's Eve. In my next letter to Andrea, I asked if she would be my date. It was the first time that I really asked her out.

I returned to Boston for the break and drove down to New Jersey, where Andrea was spending the holidays with her family. The night before New Year's Eve, I took Andrea to a movie. On New Year's Eve, we went with Henry and Chickie to a Hungarian restaurant in New York City called Chardas. I didn't go to many restaurants then, and I was somewhat unaware of what the cost might be. I never had a lot of money anyway. The bill for dinner was fifty dollars per couple and I had only thirty dollars in my pocket. I borrowed money from Henry to pay for dinner as well as a little more for gas to get home.

After the winter break, I returned to Chicago for the remainder of the year. Andrea and I continued to correspond. When I left law school and returned to Boston, we began dating seriously.

Before winter break, I had taken the first trimester exams. I received my marks when I returned. I did very well in four of my five courses. In the fifth course, which was on contracts, I did very poorly.

When he passed back our graded exams, the professor of the course, Malcolm Sharp, made an announcement. "Anybody who doesn't like or understand their mark can come see me."

I made an appointment to see Professor Sharp. I was hoping that he could explain what I had misunderstood about the material on the exam.

Professor Sharp said, "Look, Mr. Leven, you don't understand what this is all about, and I'm not sure you'll ever understand it."

I had expected that he would walk me through the exam and explain my errors so that I could learn from my mistakes and improve. Instead, he essentially said, "You'll never get it." He destroyed me.

I didn't know what to do. I had never failed. I completely fell apart. I went back to my dorm and told Richard Bogosian what had happened. "I'm going to leave," I said. "There is no reason for me to stay. I guess I don't understand the material. I'll never be a good lawyer, so I might as well give up."

"You can't do that," Richard said. He tried to convince me otherwise.

But I had made up my mind. I was leaving. I sold my books back to the bookstore. Then I wrote a letter to my parents telling them that I was leaving school and explaining why. I knew that it would take me a few days to drive home, and I wanted the letter to arrive before I did so that my parents had some warning.

Then I got a phone call. Richard had gone to the dean and told him that I was going to leave.

The dean of the law school at that time was Edward Levy, who later became an attorney general of the United States. I agreed to meet with him.

"Why are you leaving?" Dean Levy asked me.

I told him the story.

He asked me to stay. "Stay one year. Stay until the end of the first year."

"Dean," I said, "I'm going home." I was shattered by my failure in the course and the response of Professor Sharp. Also, I was lonely and homesick. The University of Chicago's law school just didn't feel right. I wanted to return to Boston.

Decades later, in a business meeting, I bumped into a man named Levy. "You're not related to Edward Levy are you?" I asked.

"He was my father," the man answered.

I said, "Let me tell you a story." I told him about Professor Malcolm Sharp.

"I'm not surprised," Edward Levy's son said. "He was a horrible person. He destroyed more people than you."

On the nineteen-hour drive home that winter from Chicago to Boston, I worried about how my parents would react. They had hoped that I would be the first lawyer in the family. I thought that they might tell me to go back to school, or at least express their disappointment. I arrived home in the evening, parked the car, walked up the sidewalk, and knocked on the door. My father answered. I didn't know what to say.

"Welcome home," my father said and brought me into the house. He never so much as questioned my decision.

I realize now that I probably would not have been a good lawyer. The way that I decided to leave was not ideal, but the result was probably for the best.

When I went to see my mother, she asked, "What are you going to do with yourself?"

"I'll find something to do," I said confidently. "I'll go to graduate school. Boston University is down the street." The next week I went to Boston University and got the catalog. The College of Communications had a one-year graduate program in public relations. I applied and was accepted.

MORGAN MEMORIAL

While I was studying public relations, I took a part-time job at Morgan Memorial Goodwill Home for Boys, a residential program for troubled young men. The facility housed about fifteen boys aged fifteen and sixteen who were sent by their parents because of behavioral issues at home or at school. There was a mixture of African American and Caucasian kids, those from wealthy families, and those from economically disadvantaged backgrounds.

I worked for a dollar and a quarter an hour for thirty hours a week in the afternoons after my graduate school classes. My job was to assist with the care of the boys. It was not unlike being a counselor at Camp Tevya, except at Morgan Memorial, I was working with kids who needed help as opposed to working with kids from privileged backgrounds. I took the kids to the park to play softball, or I sat and talked with them. One time I was boxing with one of the kids, and he nearly killed me with a left jab—I didn't know how to box, and he obviously did. My duties were loosely structured, and as with many of the jobs that I'd had up until then and would have going forward, there was no formal training or instruction. I assessed the situations as they arose, decided on the best way to respond, asked for assistance when needed, and did what needed to be done. When there was nothing for me to do with the kids, I went to the office and read their file jackets so that I could learn something about them.

At Morgan Memorial, I worked with two African American men who both held PhDs: John Moreland and Bernard Pendleton. John Moreland ran the home. He was an enormous man who had played tackle for the Grambling football team and had once been married to the daughter of A. Philip Randolph, the head of the Sleeping Car Porters Union and a major civil rights leader. Moreland had written a book about the civil rights movement called *Unrest*. When I was first hired, John Moreland called me into his office. He had a deep, booming voice. "Mr. Leven," he said to me, "you're going to learn a lot of things here because you've never worked for a black man before."

It was 1960 and still a rare thing for an African American to have achieved PhD status. To me, the boss was the boss, regardless of race. I really respected John Moreland and loved my job at Morgan Memorial, but working with Moreland and Pendleton constantly reminded me of how unjust the world could be. At one point, Pendleton needed an apartment, and there was a sign advertising a vacancy in the complex across the street from me. "I can't move there," Pendleton told me. "It's Brookline. They won't take me because I'm black."

I worked at the home for a year until I graduated with my master's degree in public relations and communications. At the end of the year, John Moreland offered me a permanent position. "I'll pay for you to get a master's degree in social work," he told me. "I'll give you a dollar and a half an hour."

If I hadn't met Andrea and if we hadn't already been talking about getting married, I might very well have hung around. I really enjoyed the job. I'd always thought about becoming a camp director someday or owning my own camp, and becoming a social worker seemed like a step in that direction. But Andrea and I were already very serious. I knew that I couldn't support a family on a dollar and a half an hour.

I turned down Moreland's job offer and began looking for a position in public relations. I asked Moreland if he would write me a letter of reference.

To Whom It May Concern:

It gives me a great deal of pleasure to recommend to you Michael A. Leven.

This young man came to work with us about a year ago, and during this period has contributed a great deal to the efficiency of our unit. However, there are several intangibles beyond efficiency which have accrued to us in consequence of his presence.

1. He is a jovial, personable, and intelligent fellow.

2. He has been found to be circumspect in his dealing with all members of our organization.

3. He has made up for a lack of experience by initiative, desire, and, in short, hard and thoughtful work.

4. He has put his heart into the job at all times.
Mr. Leven will be an asset to anyone whether in an employment or a social situation.

Lastly, I can only say Mr. Leven's presence will be very much missed. This young man has an excellent future in store for him. His executive potential is paramount. Thank you.

Sincerely Yours,
   J. B. Moreland

I still have that letter today and am still amazed by it. I was twenty-three at the time and still figuring myself out, yet he seemed to know me and what I was capable of. He saw that I put my heart into my work and recognized the ways that this counterpoised my inexperience. The letter was predictive of what I would achieve. Part of great leadership is being able to understand people and to see the strengths and potential that even they don't realize.

I never saw John Moreland again. I tried to find him some years later but had no success. There was no trace of him or even of the book that he had written.

FREE LUNCH

My final thesis in graduate school was on institutional advertising. I conducted research by sending out questionnaires to several advertising agencies and public relations firms and compiling the data that they sent back. I was interested in the project, but moreover, it seemed like a possible path to getting a job.

That spring I sent out over fifty résumés to firms in Boston, New York, and New Jersey—places where Andrea and I had some foundation. I didn't get one job offer or even an interview. I later found out that you could only be hired in public relations if you had previous experience working for a newspaper. There were two training programs in New York at advertising agencies: one was in media buying and the other was in management training. If you were Jewish, however, organizations wouldn't accept you into the management training programs because they didn't want to expose you to the clients. My options were limited.

I didn't have lofty goals back then. I wanted to finish college, find a job, get married, and have kids. Now I was months away from getting married, and I had no money and no job. I went to the Boston University job placement office. It wasn't much of an office back then, but they were helpful. They found a job opening in New York City: sales promotion manager of the Hotel Roosevelt. The job paid $5,100 a year and free lunch. I applied.

The hotel was leased by a company in Boston called Hotel Corporation of America, which later changed its name to Sonesta Corporation, so although the hotel was in New York, my first stop toward getting the job was in Boston. I got an interview with a man in the personnel department named Jack Hawley, and we hit it off right away. He went over my education, my background as a counselor, and my other achievements. "You're terrific," he told me in the interview. "You'd be perfect."

I didn't even know what a sales promotion manager did, but I knew that I needed a job, and I was confident that I could learn.

"You've got to go to New York for an interview," Jack Hawley told me.

In New York, I had an interview with the personnel director, Ed Rogers. He agreed with Jack Hawley. "You'll be terrific," he said.

Finally, I asked, "What does the sales promotion manager do?"

He offered a list of tasks. "You change the signs in the lobby and the elevators. You create the brochures, do things to promote the hotel."

That sounded simple enough. He hired me.

I would report to the sales director, and in addition to my salary and free lunch, if I worked for the company for forty years, I would get a pension of forty dollars a month.

"I don't expect I'm going to stay for forty years," I told Ed Rogers, "but that all sounds good."

I didn't know anything about the hotel industry. I'd only stayed at hotels twice: Lord Balfour in Miami when I was a child and traveling with my family and once as a junior in college. I didn't pause to think that I might be getting in over my head. I needed a job, and I was confident that I could learn.

A MAY WEDDING

Andrea and I were married in May 1961 after Andrea graduated from Boston University. Everyone gets married in June, and I wanted to be different. We were married in a synagogue in Teaneck, New Jersey, that was large enough to accommodate the wedding that my father-in-law wanted for his daughter. My father-in-law owned a five-and-ten store, which meant that my in-laws were not rich but comfortable. I remember Andrea's mother asking me before the wedding, "Do you think you can keep my daughter in the style to which she's accustomed?" I had no idea what style she was talking about. I was in trouble if the wedding was an example of how they wanted me to provide for their daughter.

Over two hundred guests attended the wedding. Several of my fraternity brothers were there with their wives, along with my grandmother and many of my aunts and uncles. The wedding party wore top hats and tails—I had hair then and looked strange in a top hat. Andrea looked gorgeous. There was a big band, catering, dancing, and eating. It was a great party.

My mother was relatively uncomfortable with how big and expensive the wedding was. She hadn't been to many weddings like that. My parents were quite conservative with how they spent money and what they displayed publicly. I remember my mother saying to me after I got engaged, "You better be sure of this. Because I'm not sure you can live in this environment."

Andrea did come from a higher economic class than my parents and I were from. It was a bit of a different world for me and for my parents. But my parents were amazingly flexible and adaptable. My mother especially had an incredible ability to be comfortable with anyone. She could be with kings and queens or with the poorest people on the block. My father also had friends at every level of lifestyle. That is one of the gifts that I was given from my parents—I have a broad comfort zone when it comes to associating with other people. I've worked for billionaires and disadvantaged youth, in all sorts of different situations, with people of all shapes, sizes, and kinds. It's not only a tolerance for difference but also a true capacity to connect to others—something that feels innate.

My wife is the same way. Her family was better off than mine, but they had friends both from higher and from lower social statuses. My in-laws were very good to their family members who were less fortunate.

Although my mother could be comfortable anywhere, she did worry whether I would be. But I was the child of my parents in that regard—easily moving within social circles. Andrea and I passed that way of being in the world on to our own children, who also socialize effortlessly with all sorts of people. While our wedding was lavish, it was also fun. People had a good time. They moved around the dance floor together, conversed over food and drinks, and enjoyed themselves and one another. It was a glimpse of how Andrea and I would embrace our shared future.

Lessons Learned

16. Be aware that it is easy to destroy someone with a simple remark. Never take another's dignity away.

17. Even when disappointed by a situation or the behavior of another, you can still be compassionate.

18. Do your homework. What you discover will be of value later.

19. Discrimination is pervasive; it is always there.

20. People are the same regardless of race, gender, religion, and other classifications. You should never be apprehensive about being employed by or employing someone who looks different from you.

21. Others may see in you things that you do not want to see in yourself.

PART II

EXPERIENCE AS
EStory EDUCATION

CHAPTER 4

SALES, 1961–1964

THE CLUB BAR

Months before Andrea and I were married and moved to New York, I started my job at the Roosevelt. The Roosevelt is located across from Grand Central Station. Aside from more than eight hundred rooms, it also holds meeting spaces, ballrooms, restaurants, and bars. When I worked there, the hotel was leased by the Hotel Corporation of America, a company that managed many hotels around the country. I started at ninety-eight dollars a week plus free lunch, which I usually ate at a table mostly filled with World War II vets. These other employees were closer to my father's age than to mine, but they were incredibly hospitable and good advisers.

As sales promotion manager, I did the range of duties that Ed Rogers had promised, including changing signs in the hotel displays. The Roosevelt Hotel had a bar off the lobby called the Club Car Bar. Because the hotel was connected to Grand Central Station, a lot of people passed through when they took the shortcut through the tunnel to the station. In the two windows on either side of the door to the bar—the windows that hundreds of people passed each day—the Roosevelt had put out fake flowers. The decor didn't make a lot of sense to me for a bar named the Club Car that was located next to a train station.

I went down to the Lionel Trains office in the Empire State Building and introduced myself to the receptionist. "Hi, I'm Mike Leven, the sales promotion manager at the Roosevelt Hotel. I'd like to get some train cars to display in the windows of the Club Car Bar … a caboose, an engine … something to put in the window. Could you lend me some model trains?"

A big box arrived on my desk a day later containing six train cars. I took the plastic flowers out and put the train cars in. They looked great. Lionel Trains was getting a little free advertising, and the Roosevelt was getting decor suitable for the Club Car Bar.

The next day a man named Mr. Vas Diaz wanted to see me. He was the controller. I had no idea what a controller was and was told by the office manager of the sales and banquet department, Helen Quinn, that it was somewhat like an accountant. I went up to see Mr. Vas Diaz in his office and introduced myself.

Mr. Vas Diaz shifted in his seat and stared at me. "Did you take the flowers out of the window downstairs?" he asked me.

"Yes, sir. I did," I told him. "It's the Club Car Bar, and I thought it ought to have some trains."

"I don't know who you are or what you do," he said in a tone that was distinctly irate rather than congratulatory. "I put those flowers in the window and you took them out."

I stood my ground. "No insult to you," I said. "I think this is the right thing to do."

"You better stay clear of me," he warned. "Now get out of my office."

That was my welcome by a senior executive at the Roosevelt Hotel. I could have asked more questions before I made the change, but even if I had done so, I would have likely stepped on his toes at some later point. I hadn't meant to insult anyone, but more importantly, I thought that the change was a good decision. It isn't possible to always avoid conflict.

I ended up having small conflicts with people in accounting and finance departments my entire career. I once went to a speech given by the human resources director of Disney. He was talking about accountants and he said, "If Thomas Edison had been an accountant, all we'd have today is a longer candle." I've used that quote in several speeches I've given since. Accountants tend to view the world and business through a different lens than do I. Often accountants are so focused on an end goal that they are unable to think tangentially or creatively or to consider other aspects of a job, like marketing. Somewhere down the line, Mr. Vas Diaz likely learned that flowers were the appropriate decoration for windows. He couldn't think outside of that narrow decision to consider what was best for the specific situation: the Club Car Bar.

I never doubted the decision. The trains stayed in the windows for twenty years—long after I was gone—until the name of the bar changed.

MY FIRST BOOKING

A week later, the sales director, Larry de Francis, called to tell me that the Roosevelt was eliminating the job of sales promotion manager. "We want you to go to the sales department," he said.

It was the third week of February, and I was getting married in May. I needed to have a job, so I agreed.

"You'll be fine," he said. He assured me that I would be trained.

The next day I came to work as a salesman. I was given a desk, a secretary, and a mentor named Lou Fiora—another World War II vet—who would train me.

I shadowed Lou Fiora for a couple of days. My job would be to book rooms, both the standard hotel rooms and the meeting and event spaces. Lou took me through his daily routine of making solicitation calls in the morning and showing the spaces to customers in the afternoon. "When you're showing a room to a customer," Lou told me, "you ask the front desk for a few keys. Then you let the customer pick the key so that they know you're not fooling them with the only good room."

Two weeks later, Larry de Francis was fired—he wasn't very good at his job. It was March 1961.

The new sales director was named Joe McCarthy. He was an Irish Catholic from Boston, very bright and self-made. McCarthy called me into his office with some bad news. "Mike," he said, "we have two new salespeople here. I have to lay off one of you."

The other salesperson was a guy named Tom Cunningham, who had been working in the front office of the Essex House Hotel for the past couple of years and knew the hotel business inside and out, but like me, he was new to sales. Joe McCarthy told me that he was going to take both Tom and me out on sales calls and, based on our performances on those calls, would make a decision about who to keep.

One of the things that I had going for me was that Tom Cunningham was fairly boring. I don't know how his day out with Joe went, but I imagine they didn't have much to talk about. I had a fairly average sales day when Joe took me out. I stayed in the routine that Lou Fiori had taught me. I had no idea what choice Joe was going to make. I was getting married in a few months. I needed the job.

Joe called me into his office. "You've got the job," he told me.

Shortly thereafter, there was a sales meeting. There was a pending crisis that could harm the hotel: jet planes were replacing prop planes. The Roosevelt Hotel's clientele mainly came by train through Grand Central Station that serviced people arriving to New York from all over the country. By train, a trip could not be made to New York City in one day, thereby necessitating that people stay an extra night in New York. Jet planes, however, would offer a much quicker trip. Visitors would therefore not need to stay additional nights. The Roosevelt viewed jet planes as a threat to business.

I have always thought differently from other people, and I have always been gifted with an ability to see the angles of situations that are not recognized by others. "It is inevitable that the jet planes will become popular," I said, "so isn't there a way for us to take advantage of their availability?"

Years later I came across a speech by then-governor of New York Martin Van Buren, who spoke out against railroads, citing a fear that the trains would put current transportation—horse-drawn boats on the Erie Canal—out of business. Van Buren saw this change from travel by boat to train as a hindrance rather than as the opportunity history proved it to be. The railroads may have forced some boat captains to find other work, but it ultimately brought far more business to New York City. In the same way, it seemed that we would likely need to make changes in consideration of people traveling by jet plane but that jet planes would ultimately bring more business to the hotel. My suggestion was not unlike my replacement of the flowers in the window of the Club Car Bar with model trains: the other salespeople were resistant to my suggestions at first.

As promised, Joe McCarthy trained me in sales. He gave me a more set routine than Lou Fiora had provided. He told me to arrive at 8:00 a.m., plan five personal sales calls for the morning, invite a customer to join me for lunch, and go out again in the afternoon and make five more personal sales calls. At 4:00 p.m., I would return to my office to write reports about my calls and then bring the reports to Joe at 5:00 p.m. so that we could discuss my day. "If you do that every day for the next seven or eight months," Joe told me, "you'll be the leading salesperson in the Roosevelt Hotel."

Hotels make their money on a combination of booking rooms to guests—the highest margin of profitability—and booking banquets to businesses and events that earn profits in food and beverage as well as the bookings. Convention hotels combine these two profit streams, selling banquet space to the convention organization and selling rooms to the convention participants. The Roosevelt was a convention hotel, especially hosting a lot of banquets.

Major hotels have both marketing and sales departments. Marketing departments combine public relations and targeted advertising to market the hotel and promote the hotel's image to potential and existing customers. Sales departments focus on the actual sale to the customer. In the 1960s, however, marketing departments did not exist. The sales department did it all.

As a salesperson at the Roosevelt, I started with what are referred to as dead accounts. These were customers—association conventions, corporations, travel companies, and other businesses—that had used the hotel in the past but who hadn't given the hotel any business for years. I worked the routine that Joe had given me, going out to these businesses to make personal calls.

More often than not, I showed up to the addresses on file to find that the companies had gone out of business. At that time, leads were kept in a Diebold file system that held countless index cards reporting on organizations with whom the hotel had or could possibly do business. I would be given a pile of these accounts from the sales office and then would go to the addresses to find that the businesses were no longer there, or had changed management, or had evolved into another type of business altogether. Several cards also had three *X*s on them. Joe McCarthy explained that the accounts with three *X*s could only be booked for time in July and August.

"Why?" I asked.

"Because those are black associations."

Hotels did very minimal business in July and August.

For the most part, the accounts in the Diebold file were dead accounts and therefore useless leads. I needed to create my own accounts. I began to make phone calls to area businesses. When that led nowhere, I went to competing hotels and read their billboards. Hotels used to display the list of meetings and events that they were hosting on billboards. I began calling the companies in those listings—companies that I knew were currently making bookings—and pitching the Roosevelt. Nine months later, just as Joe McCarthy had predicted, I was the leading salesperson at the Roosevelt.

The New York Savings Bank Association was one company that I discovered on a billboard in another hotel. The bank association was managed by a man named Bodine.

"It's funny you're here," Mr. Bodine said when I made a personal call to his office. "I need a luncheon for sixty people next week."

"Our Madison Room holds sixty people," I told him. I quoted him the price of $4.20 per person for lunch. "I need to check on the availability," I said.

I walked the few blocks back to the Roosevelt and went to the banquet department to check on the availability of the Madison Room. The banquet department was run by a man named Herb Erman who reserved the room for me. I walked back to New York Savings Bank and told Mr. Bodine that his luncheon was scheduled.

"Great," Mr. Bodine said, but he had a request: he wanted ten tables of six.

I walked back to the Roosevelt to talk the Herb again. "We don't do ten tables of six," Herb told me. "It's got to be tables of eight."

I went back to the New York Savings Bank and told Mr. Bodine, "I can't do ten tables of six."

"Why?" Mr. Bodine asked.

I didn't know.

"Mr. Leven," he said, "how long have you been doing this?"

I told him that I'd just started a couple of months ago.

"I'm the customer," he told me. "I want tables of six. Do you understand?"

I did understand. "I'm going to make it happen for you," I told Mr. Bodine.

I went back to the Roosevelt and asked Herb why he couldn't host tables of six. "The union has to have tables of eight," he told me. "They get more gratuity for a table of eight."

The problem seemed simple, as did the solution. I returned to Mr. Bodine and told him that the tables of six would cost him slightly more—to make up for the lost gratuity.

"You got a deal," Mr. Bodine said. He got his tables of six, and the banquet staff got their gratuity. That was my first booking.

Mr. Bodine reminded me of a factor important to all business: the company serves the customers. From that first sale at the Roosevelt, this has been my mantra. Bureaucracy often gets in the way of the customer's needs. It is the job of people in sales to seek solutions to ensure that the customer is served. I built a reputation for making things

> It is the job of people in sales to seek solutions to ensure that the customer is served.

work for the customer, and based on this reputation, I received a lot of repeat business.

THE ROOSEVELT

The salespeople working for the companies who book meetings and conventions are solicited by dozens of hotels. They meet with many representatives, like me, who try to sign their accounts. I knew that to be successful, I needed to stand out. I once called on sales manager Jack Troy at Pfizer twenty-seven times, trying to get him to take a meeting with me about booking space at the Roosevelt. On the twenty-seventh time I went to see him, he agreed. "I figured I might as well see you this time," he told me. My persistence had made me stand out from the crowd.

Most of what I learned about sales and working in business, I learned through experience. Very seldom did anyone teach me anything directly—as Joe McCarthy had. Instead, I studied what other people did. I had also learned a lot growing up with my father and hearing stories about his job. My father really loved his customers. He enjoyed spending time with them and thought of them as family. He made every relationship personal, and I took that perspective with me into my professional life.

I especially remember a conversation that I had with Herb Teeple, who organized the events for the Technical Association of the Pulp and Paper Industry (TAPPI). TAPPI was a big account, and Herb was a larger-than-life figure. He was very professional and used to smoke a pipe. I met him for lunch one day, hoping to convince him to bring his business to the Hotel Corporation of America. Lunch meetings are complicated; they are both business and social. While both parties are representing their companies, the fact that you are out of the office and sharing a meal means that there will be small talk or personal conversation that veers away from the business at hand. At this lunch meeting, I asked Herb all about the paper industry. I wanted to know everything: Where did the pulp come from? How was it made? How did different types of pulp change the final result? He talked through lunch about the mechanics of making and selling paper. At the end of the meal, he said to me, "This has been the best lunch I've ever had with any hotel salesperson. All the rest only wanted to talk about Mickey Mantle's batting average. You asked about what's important to me."

"I was really interested," I said sincerely. "Thank you for talking to me. And by the way, Mantle's average is three fourteen."

> To make a successful sale, salespeople need to get to know the customer as a person.

Herb and I became friends, much in the way that my dad had become friends with his customers. At the end of the day, a sale is a relationship that will only be as successful as the connection between the buyer and the seller. The salesperson must build a relationship with the customer, and to do that, you must get to know the customer: their situation, what they want, what's important to them. It's not about what you're selling.

Later, when I was training my own salespeople, I emphasized the importance of having empathy for the person on the other side of the table. To make a successful sale, salespeople need to get to know the customer as a person.

ONE OF US

Very early in my career at the Roosevelt, I made up my mind that I had to get support from the various departments in the hotel: the service department, the food and beverage department, the banquet department, and so on. I worked to build relationships with the people who had responsibility in those departments—the people who would be taking care of my customers. When I had a free lunch, I ate with them. I made a point of moving around in the hotel rather than separating myself in my office. I spent time asking questions and expressing interest in their work. I offered to help in ways that I could. I made a point of knowing as many people at the Roosevelt as I could.

The working environment at the Roosevelt was generally cordial, although it's worth noting that it was also very homogenous. I was one of only two Jewish people working in the hotel. It was the sort of thing that I took notice of only a couple of times.

One time was when I went to shoot pool with Bill Spanton. Bill Spanton had been a sergeant in World War II. He wore a dead Nazi's ring on his finger, and when asked about it, Bill would tell the story of cutting the ring off the dead German's finger. He was a very tough guy. He liked me because my father was also a World War II veteran. Bill and I waited at the same bus terminal when we went home in the evenings and often talked.

One day on the way home, Bill asked me if I wanted to shoot pool. I had played pool a bit as a kid but hadn't played for years. "I'm not much of a player," I told him, "but sure, I can play."

He took me to a place called McGirr's Pool Room on Eighth Avenue. While we were shooting pool, he said, "Hey, Mike, can I ask you a question? Why do you people work so hard?"

It took me a moment to realize that by "you people" he meant Jewish people, specifically me and Ed Rogers from human resources—the only other Jewish person at the Roosevelt.

"I don't think I work hard," I told Bill. "I'm just trying to get the job done."

I had been talking with Bill for months, but in that moment, it occurred to me that to him I was different in some way—the Jewish salesman at the Roosevelt rather than just another salesman.

Ed Rogers and I weren't the only ones who were thought of as different, however. The food and beverage manager at the Roosevelt was a German by the name of Hans Post. Hans was not only German but also a quintessential German: blond haired and blue eyed. If you put him in uniform, he would have looked like he worked for the Luftwaffe. He had a very heavy German accent. One day at lunch, Hans came by the table where I often ate with the officers, and one of the men said to him, "Hans, I piloted a B-25 in World War Two. I flew twenty-seven missions in Germany and dropped tons of bombs. How did I miss you?"

Much of the table laughed, but I was embarrassed. As cordial as the environment was at the Roosevelt, these kinds of insensitivities were commonplace. The veterans especially often made jokes and accosted people in these ways. Hans was around my age, and he was obviously too young to have had anything to do with the war, but the veterans saw him as German first and a coworker second. It was a tough environment in that way for anyone who was different.

Discrimination not only came from my peers but also from the customers. In 1962, I had a meeting with the head of the New York State Contractors Association, who knew an executive at the Americana Hotel, and he asked me if I would like to work there.

He called his friend, Mr. O'Reilly, and said, "I'm sitting with a great salesperson from the Roosevelt Hotel. You have any job openings?"

O'Reilly said, "Is he one of us?" meaning, is he Irish. It seemed that was a prerequisite to getting a job with the Americana Hotel.

THE PLAZA

By the end of the year, my sale of future bookings far surpassed those of all my counterparts. Joe McCarthy called me into his office again and said, "Mike, you've done a great job. I'm going to give you two options. Either I'll give you a raise from $5,100 to $6,500, or I'll give you a raise to $6,000 and promote you from sales representative to assistant sales manager."

I took the title. I left $500 on the table in exchange for a position that I hoped would accelerate my career and make it easier for me to make sales. I was playing the long game.

My responsibilities were exactly the same as assistant sales manager as they had been when I was a sales representative. After a year, I was still the leading salesperson at the Roosevelt. Then, in 1962, an opportunity arose with the Hotel Corporation of America. Terry Rufer, the New York area sales manager, was promoted to director of sales of the Plaza Hotel in New York. In the position of New York area sales manager, he had booked all the hotels owned by the Hotel Corporation of America, now called Sonesta.

I went to Joe McCarthy and told him that I wanted the New York area sales manager position.

"You're too important to the Roosevelt," he told me. "I can't let you go."

In January 1963, I got a call from a sales manager with the International Playtex Corporation. It was a relatively small and somewhat unknown company back then, limited to the sale of bras and girdles. A year earlier, I had found their name on the billboard at another hotel, solicited the sales manager, and booked their account. Since then, I had had regular meetings with the sales manager. I assumed that he wanted to make a booking.

"We have a job opening for a sales director for small stores in Westchester and the Bronx," the sales manager told me. The job paid $12,000 a year and included a car. I was interested, and after an interview, I was offered the job.

I told Joe McCarthy that I had been given another offer and was planning to leave. "I just want you to know," I told him, "you've been great to me."

"You can't leave," Joe said. "I want Earl Duffy to talk to you."

Earl Duffy was the national sales manager for the Hotel Corporation of America. Joe called and arranged for him to come to New York the following day to talk with me.

My father happened to be in New York at the time on business, and we had dinner together. I told him about the offer with Playtex and the upcoming meeting with Earl Duffy. My father's response was, "I don't know what Earl Duffy's going to say to you, but I don't think you ought to be selling bras and girdles. Bras and girdles, what's that?" It didn't seem then that Playtex was going to grow into the internationally recognized company that it is today. A move to Playtex seemed like a move from a well-respected and established business to a company and business that was less secure.

"We'll see," I told my father.

The next day Earl Duffy offered me the New York area sales manager job for the Hotel Corporation of America—Terry Rufer's old position and the one for which I had asked Joe McCarthy to be considered. The job paid $7,700 a year. I would work in an office next to the Plaza and, along with three other area sales managers throughout the country, represent all the hotels in the company.

My father was certain that I should stay in the hotel business. "That's the business for you," he told me.

I felt like I'd made the right decision when I called the sales manager at Playtex to tell him that I couldn't accept his offer, and rather than congratulate me on my promotion, or try to convince me otherwise, or tell me he hoped that we could remain in business together, he hung up without saying a word.

I moved to the building next door to the Plaza and began representing potential accounts in the New York area and Philadelphia. There were four national salespeople in the Hotel Corporation of America, including locations in New York, Boston, Chicago, and Washington. Each month a $100 bonus was awarded to the national salesperson who brought in the most business. I won the $100 my first month in sales and then won every month for the next sixteen months. My seventeenth month, the company awarded $100 to all four salespeople because the contest was becoming so discouraging to the other national salespeople. I likely would have done fine at Playtex, but ultimately the New York area sales director position was the right decision for me. The hospitality business treated me well for the next decades.

The New York area sales manager job was an important position for me not only because I gained experience but also because I gained the exposure of having a corporate job. I was no longer working for one hotel but representing an entire organization. I met a wider spectrum of people and had better opportunities. When Earl Duffy recognized my potential, he sent me to national training sessions where I met more people in the hospitality business and built an even wider range of relationships.

Lessons Learned

22. Take the time to explain decisions and help people to understand what you want them to do. You may see things they don't, or they may be afraid to ask questions. (Often people with the most experience have difficulty with what they don't understand.)

23. When hiring, do not look only at technical competence; look at the entire person.

24. When you are successful in a particular job, often the boss will deter you from going to another.

25. The customer is not always right but is always the customer.

26. Find a way around procedures that could prevent customer satisfaction.

27. Persistence is the most important characteristic for salespeople.

28. Get to know your customer. Understanding their interests, which may be different from yours, is key to making the right sale.

29. You are not alone in an organization. Get to know your peers, understand them, and be a part of the team.

30. Don't move from one company (or one job) to another for money. Move when the opportunity provides a chance to learn something new.

CHAPTER 5

OPERATIONS, 1965–1969

T-GROUP TRAINING

In 1963, I was promoted to regional sales manager of the Hotel Corporation of America, which owned the Roosevelt, the Plaza, and several other hotels. While in that position, they changed their name to Sonesta. I worked in New York then, but Andrea and I lived in an apartment in New Jersey, close to where Andrea taught high school. I spent a lot of my time in my office next to the Plaza, but I also traveled by train every six weeks to Philadelphia to touch base with the companies there with whom we worked.

Eventually I was recognized as a high-potential employee and invited to management training meetings. One of those meetings was a T-Group training, which focused on interactions and problem-solving activities between people from different disciplines. The purpose was to help participants gain insights about themselves and their own roles in the company. At the T-Group training, I met Dick Bromley, the general manager of the Kenmore Hotel in Boston. We got along well and would stay in touch for years to come.

As part of the training session, I was put into a group with people from accounting, food and beverage, rooms, general management, maintenance, and other departments. We were given a problem to solve together over the course of a week. At the end of the week, each group selected one group member to present the group's solution. Often, people from the sales department were selected to represent their groups because we had good communication skills and experience making presentations. For these reasons, I was chosen to represent my group.

Each group representative presented with their groups seated behind them. The leaders of the training suggested that before the presenters answered audience questions, they might want to consult with their group. I followed this suggestion, and it compromised my presentation.

"That's the worst presentation I've seen in all the years I've been facilitating these trainings," the T-Group training organizer told me after my presentation. He said that I was trying so hard to involve the other people in my group that I forgot who I was. My own voice and opinions were lost.

He gave me some advice: "Be who you are and don't try to be anybody you're not."

It was simple when spoken but complicated in practice. It is difficult within a group dynamic to balance the needs and perspectives of the group while maintaining your own judgments and goals. It was something that I had not thought about directly before then, and it ultimately became a major learning experience. While this is challenging for people in all positions in a company, it is especially challenging for salespeople, who often are the face of the company. As was true for the T-Group training exercise, it is the salespeople who address the public and who must balance an intimate interpersonal interaction with an approved representation of the company as a whole; they must be both professional and personal. To successfully build relationships with other institutions, they must be the company and also be themselves. In the T-Group training, I had forgotten to also be myself. Because of this, I did not connect with the audience and offer a succinct view of our group's solution.

Even during the next years, when I moved away from sales, my experience in sales benefited me greatly. Many organizations disregarded the sales department. In the early days of the hospitality business, sales was often the last department to be formed. Non-convention hotels didn't have sales departments at all—organizations didn't feel that they were really necessary. In my early days in hospitality, the front office controlled bookings and worked directly with the banquet department to help customers organize meetings—work that sales departments would do later. When sales departments did exist, they were often left out of the company's larger plan.

In the following decades of my career, as I moved into positions with more responsibility and authority, and as the hospitality business became more competitive, sales departments became more important. I came to understand all the ways that sales departments could make a difference in the overall success of an organization, and I worked to build the sales departments of the companies for whom I was employed.

> Remember, no matter how great the market is doing, nothing happens in a business until somebody makes a sale.

Even when I wasn't managing the sales department per se (when I was working in operations and more invested in analysis and the accounting side of the business), I spent a great deal of time connecting with the people who worked in those departments. I made sure to honor the salespeople. I never forgot that the sales department was critical to the success of the company. Remember, no matter how great the market is doing, nothing happens in a business until somebody makes a sale.

THE KENMORE

While I was making my way at Sonesta, Andrea was fired from her job teaching Spanish at Cliffside Park High School in New Jersey after she caught a student cheating on a final exam and gave the student a failing mark. The student's family was politically connected. The school pressured Andrea to change the grade. Andrea refused—my wife is a principled person; we share these values.

Andrea got another job almost immediately, working for North Bergen High School, where she would make $4,700 a year. I was making $7,700 a year. We were moving up the scale financially. It was 1963.

By January, I was responsible for selling major accounts for Sonesta; these were accounts for large associations, conventions, and corporations that could hold business meetings at any of the Sonesta hotels around the United States—the Mayflower in Washington, the Royal Orleans in New Orleans, the Kenmore in Boston—and in resort areas in Bermuda, the Bahamas, and Puerto Rico. These were not the dead accounts that I had been given as a younger salesperson at the Roosevelt; these were accounts with well-established businesses, professional associations, and travel managers with a national presence. This made the job easier: I was able to research these organizations and connect more easily with the people within them, but the demands on me were increased. I now had to understand the facilities and the capacities of all the hotels that I was representing around the country and beyond. My schedule was crowded with traveling to Philadelphia every six weeks by train to make cold calls; working in New York City, Westchester, and other places in the region where there were corporations that might be willing to bring their business to Sonesta; and studying the marketplace. I reported to the national sales manager, Earl Duffy, in Boston. By the end of 1963, I had a very good national exposure.

One hundred dollars was awarded each month to the leading salesperson among the four sales offices: Washington, Chicago, Boston, and New York. When I had been the New York area sales manager for Sonesta for seventeen months, I saw an ad in the *New York Times* for a director of sales and catering at the Kenmore Hotel in Boston—another Sonesta Hotel—for $12,000 a year plus bonuses. The job was an opportunity to learn more about operations. Ultimately, it seemed that to really move forward, I would need a comprehensive understanding of the inner workings of hotels. Also, I knew that even though I was really good at what I was doing, I did not want to be a salesperson all my life. I called Dick Bromley, who I'd met at the T-Group training, and he offered me a job at the Kenmore Hotel.

Earl Duffy didn't want to lose me. He contacted Dick Bromley. It was a repeat of the time that I'd been offered a job by Playtex and Joe McCarthy had called Earl in a bid to hang on to me. This time, however, Dick Bromley convinced Earl to let me take the new position.

At the end of 1964, I took the job as director of sales and catering at the Kenmore. I was also an assistant to Dick Bromley.

Dick Bromley mentored me, helped me adjust to my new role, and taught me a great deal about operations. He walked the hotel with me and talked me through tasks that were completely new to me, like managing the various departments, booking bands for events, and organizing menus. My new job was at the intersection of sales and operations. I was also involved with the economics of the hotel.

CAN'T DO IT YOURSELF

A DEVASTATING DEATH

On a personal level, it was a critical time for me to be back in Boston. Because the Kenmore job started in the middle of the academic year, there were a few months when Andrea and I lived apart. I moved to Boston while Andrea stayed in New Jersey to finish her job teaching high school. Alone in Boston, I had some time on my hands and I found theater again. A friend of mine who had gone to Harvard was directing a production of *The Fantastics* and cast me in the role of the father. I was working hard then, and always at the hotel, so the music director came to the Kenmore and I rehearsed at the hotel. At the last moment, the actor cast in the lead role fell ill, and I ended up taking the lead role of El Gallo.

In June 1965, Andrea moved to Boston and into the two-bedroom apartment that I had been occupying by myself for months. That summer my parents were also moving to a new apartment in Boston, very close to where I worked. In August, my father called me at the office and said, "Your mother has passed out." He called the fire department, who in turn called an ambulance. I rushed to their house in time to see her taken away by the medical workers. She'd had a devastating stroke.

She lived for three days in the hospital, during which time my father and I did not leave her side. She was only fifty-six years old. Her own mother had died a couple of years previous, a year or two after Andrea and I were married. That had been somewhat anticipated—my grandmother had been living for years with a bad heart. But when my mother died, it was shocking and terrible. I was twenty-eight.

Her death was difficult for both my father and me, but my father absolutely fell apart—he was very connected to my mother. The transition was complicated by the move that he and my mother were in the progress of making—the new apartment not yet completely set up, the old apartment already vacated. Rather than returning to the new apartment to live alone in the rooms that he and my mother had still been furnishing, he came to live with Andrea and me.

My mother's death marked one of many big changes that happened in my personal life around that time. These incidents were both tragic and joyous and often influenced or reflected the moves that I was making in my career.

THE UNINTENTIONAL SALE OF THE KENMORE

In October, months after my mother's death, I unintentionally sold the Kenmore and eliminated my own job. An administrator for the Cambridge School for Radio and Television, a college that focused on media studies, came to see me. He wanted to buy one hundred of our rooms that he could use as dorms for his students. The Kenmore had only three hundred rooms. "Why don't you buy the whole thing?" I suggested.

He thought about it and made an offer to buy the entire hotel.

After the sale of the hotel, Sonesta transferred me to the Plaza to be director of marketing responsible for both the sales and advertising and the public relations departments. The Plaza Hotel in New York City was the most prestigious hotel in the company. Sonesta offered me an annual salary of $15,000. Before we left, Andrea and I found a one-bedroom apartment in our building in Boston for my dad and helped him move. When he was settled, we went to New York. Andrea hadn't yet found a teaching job in Boston, making the logistics of the move to New York less complicated. However, it came in the shadow of my mother's passing during a time when my father was struggling emotionally. It was a very difficult time.

I was director of marketing at the Plaza from early 1965 until late 1967. During that time, in the wake of my mother's death, my father started dating and Andrea and I had our first child. My father still worked as a traveling salesman and didn't have much money, but he was good looking and charismatic. He began to see a woman who lived in Canton, Massachusetts. Eventually he gave up his apartment in Boston and moved in with her.

In September 1966, Andrea and I had our first child—a boy. We had been married for five years and a few months. I was also becoming well known in the hospitality industry, which made my job at the Plaza easier. I liked the Plaza, but I was back in marketing and longing to be in operations—I thought that my future in the hospitality profession would depend on working in operations, preferably in a leading role—as the number two or even number one person (general manager or regional general manager) of a hotel.

RETURN TO OPERATIONS

As luck would have it, a couple of factors came together to spur my move back into operations. The first was that the president of the Plaza, Al Salomone, got another job and left. He had taught me a lot during my time at the Plaza, and I had a deep respect and admiration for him. I did not feel the same way about the man who was hired in his place, Arthur Dooley. I had met Dooley several times before when he had managed the Sonesta Hotel in Hartford, Connecticut, and I didn't have good chemistry with him. I dreaded the thought of working under him at the Plaza.

During my management training, I had met a man named Christopher Zembek, who was the general manager of Sonesta's Balmoral Beach Hotel in the Bahamas. I heard through the grapevine that he was looking for a resident manager for the hotel—a number two person. I called him.

The Balmoral Beach Hotel was a small operation with only fifty villas, but they were in the process of building 144 more rooms. It had no sales department. They needed someone who knew sales and marketing and who could act as both resident manager and assistant to the general manager. It seemed like the perfect job for me.

I took a salary cut from $15,000 to $12,000 a year, but my new salary was tax-free. The job also came with a rent-free home and full maintenance. Even with the pay cut, we were coming out ahead.

It was November 1967. My son was fifteen months old, and Andrea was pregnant with our second child, who was due in January. She couldn't come to the Bahamas until the baby was born, and so I went alone to get settled.

I missed the birth of my second son by only hours. I got the first plane out of Nassau to Miami as soon as I got word from my father-in-law that Andrea had gone to the hospital. I arrived at Saint Barnabas hospital in Newark to see her holding our second son. It was January 1968.

Six weeks later, Andrea joined me in the Bahamas with our two boys; her mother also flew down with her to help her get settled. We ensconced ourselves in the life there. It was a wonderful experience, and I got to know the travel agent, wholesaler, and airline businesses as well as the resort industry.

It was an interesting time to be working in the Bahamas. The Bahamas and Nassau had just become independent from Britain. The government was going through a transition as the island nations tried to figure out their own identities and how they wanted to be perceived on an international stage. Chris Zembek spent most of his time traveling around the world, trying to get business for the hotel. His absence meant that I was responsible for nearly all the duties at the hotel itself. Most of the previous general managers and resident managers hadn't liked the Bahamian people and had therefore kept their distance from the local community and staff. I remembered a lesson I had learned when I worked at the Kenmore Hotel, when Dick Bromley told me, "Eat in the employee dining room, talk to the hotel telephone operators, and greet the housekeeping staff in the hallways." I got to know the staff at the hotel, and they taught me the culture and customs of the Bahamas. At lunch, I ate peas and rice with the hotel employees and talked to them about their families and their lives. Although my involvement was frowned upon by the British managers who thought I was too egalitarian, I enjoyed the local community there. Knowing the people who worked in the hotel helped connect me to the hotel at large. It made me aware of the issues, challenges, and hidden strengths of the business so that I was ultimately more effective as a manager. I still believe that to be a good manager, you must know and relate to the people and business that you are managing.

In September 1968, my eldest son turned two, and Andrea and I had a birthday party for him. We had made enough friends at the hotel and in the community to host a nice group of families at our house. We had settled into the community.

One month later, in October 1968, Chris Zembek left the hotel—he did not get along well with the supervisor of the resort division in Boston. The hotel in the Bahamas would need a new general manager—a new number one. At that point, I knew the hotel inside and out. I had learned the finances, accounting, room divisions, and everything else associated with the operation of the hotel. I knew the market and the people, and the company seemed pleased with the job I was doing.

When Sonesta's Vice President of the Resort Division Robert Golbach came from Boston to assess the situation in the Bahamas, I told him that I wanted Chris Zembek's old job. Golbach looked at me sternly. "You were never a candidate," he told me. "You're just a number two guy."

Golbach replaced Zembek with his friend Manny Ferris, who was a very kind boss. Ferris moved with his family to the Bahamas, and he and his wife and Andrea and I spent a great deal of time together. Although he had taken the job that I wanted, I never resented or blamed him. We became great friends and remain friends today.

THE PRACTICING LAW INSTITUTE

Months after Manny Ferris was hired, an old friend of mine named John Monaghan, who was the vice president of sales at the Diplomat Hotel in Miami, called with a request: a customer of his named Donald Shapiro, who ran the Practicing Law Institute in New York City, was looking for meeting space in the Bahamas. "Can you take care of him?" John Monaghan asked.

"Sure," I said.

I took Donald Shapiro and his wife on a tour of the hotel and the island—by then I knew the island very well. I showed them all the tourist areas, restaurants, and beaches. At the end of his visit, Shapiro came into my office and offered me a job. "I think I'd like to have you come work for me in New York." He offered me an executive position: administrative director of the Practicing Law Institute. The salary was $22,000 and a car.

I didn't even know what the Practicing Law Institute was. I knew that they were located downtown on Wall Street and that they organized about four hundred meetings a year for lawyers. I was happy at the Balmoral Beach Hotel. Ferris was a good general manager, but I also thought that I didn't have a future with Sonesta where I wasn't seen as general manager material. I talked to Andrea. Then I talked to Ferris.

"I think you should take it," they both said.

I took the job with the Practicing Law Institute and moved my family back to New Jersey, near the office in New York City.

As administrative director of the Practicing Law Institute, I would run all the corporate meetings and manage all the executive duties; I would be responsible for all aspects of the organization except for the legal dealings. While there would be many new things to learn, my previous experience and knowledge was transferable so long as I was able to keep an open mind.

BUYING INSTEAD OF SELLING

Andrea, our two boys, and I moved back to New Jersey in 1968. We bought our first house in West Caldwell for $35,000. It was a split-level in a new development and was being constructed when we purchased it. I borrowed $2,500 from my father, $2,500 from my father-in-law, and had $2,500 in savings for a down payment. My father-in-law contributed an additional $7,000 for central air-conditioning and a crawl space. We lived with Andrea's parents for a couple of months while we waited for the construction to be completed. The house was walking distance to Bloomfield Avenue, where I could catch a bus that would take me to the Port Authority and then ride a subway to Wall Street.

My family was happy in New Jersey. Andrea enjoyed being close to her parents and siblings. My new position was not the 24/7 job that I'd held at hotels. This position was maintained within standard hours. I had more downtime. I became involved with Playcrafters, a local theater company in West Caldwell, and began to act again in plays like *The Girl in My Soup* and *A Streetcar Named Desire*.

The Practicing Law Institute was purposed on continuing education for lawyers. They held educational sessions and produced books and other training materials. I was the administrative director, and the finance department and administrative staff reported to me.

Now I was on the other side of the desk: planning meetings and calling hotels to buy space. Over the next months, I met with countless hotel salespeople—in positions like those that I had been in previously. Some were good; some were not good. I came to know the frustrations of the customer. Sometimes I would call offices and find that they had closed at five o'clock, or I would meet with people who did not have the information I needed.

In my new role, I also had the power to hire people. Fortunately, during the years that I had worked in the hospitality industry, I had met several incredible people. I hired Helen Quinn from the Roosevelt Hotel as the office administrator. I brought in someone I'd worked with at the Plaza to be the controller. This became a consistent pattern for me as a leader: I formed and maintained relationships and later brought together people who I knew, liked, and had worked well with in the past. Because my experience was extensive, I was able to build successful teams united by a singular philosophy focused on a human perspective of business: we valued people and relationships, and we strived to make connections like the ones that had brought us together.

NINETY DAYS

Things were going well at the Practicing Law Institute until one day my controller came to see me and said, "We have a problem."

The controller alleged that Shapiro might be getting payments from the book publisher in Michigan. For each of the instructional courses that the Practicing Law Institute held, participants purchased supplemental books that we produced. The Practicing Law Institute developed hundreds of different books annually that were printed by a company in Michigan. Allegedly, Shapiro had made a deal with the printing company whereby they overcharged the company for the printing and gave Shapiro the difference. In those days, such practices were not that unusual. Still, it meant that Shapiro may have been stealing from the company.

"There's more," the controller said. Shapiro had been using the company expense account to finance the redecorating of his home, specifically the refinishing of a bathroom.

I went home that day and said to Andrea, "I can't stay at the Practicing Law Institute if this funny business is going on." I was worried that Shapiro would be caught and get into trouble eventually and that I would be in trouble with him. Whistleblowing really didn't exist then. My choices were to stay knowing what Shapiro was doing, or leave. "I think I'm going to quit."

It was a good job, and I had two kids to support. The Practicing Law Institute had a TIAA, a wealth plan, a pension plan, and good benefits. Employees who worked there for forty years could retire well. But I couldn't stay.

I went to see Shapiro. I didn't accuse him of anything or even mention that I knew about his unethical dealings. "I don't want to be here anymore," I told him. Then I offered this excuse: "I want to go back to the hotel business. I miss it, and I think it's a better career for me going forward."

Shapiro didn't want me to leave. He offered me a raise from $22,000 a year to $35,000 a year. "Go home and think about it," he said.

I went home and talked to Andrea. Thirty-five thousand dollars a year was a lot of money. "I can't do it. I just can't stay," I told her. I was afraid that my reputation would be damaged beyond repair or that I would be made complicit somehow in Shapiro's business—just knowing about what was going on made me complicit on some level. "I don't think it's right," I told Andrea.

"If you want to quit, quit," Andrea said. I had her blessing.

I didn't have a plan, or much money in the bank, but I figured I could get a job. I had a good reputation from my work at the Plaza and at other places. It was a risk, but it was one I felt I had to take.

I went back to Shapiro and told him that I was going to quit.

"Do me one favor," he said. "Give me ninety days' notice so that I have time to replace you."

I agreed to give him ninety days. I began sending out applications to open positions but got no replies. I was getting nervous.

On the eighty-ninth day after I put in my resignation—one day before I would be unemployed—I got a call from Sonesta. They had heard that I was on the market and asked me to return as the international sales director for the resorts and the European hotels. They offered me the same amount of money I was making currently: $22,000 a year. I would be based in New York next to the Plaza—Andrea and I wouldn't need to move. I accepted the offer.

I later found out that Ferris had recommended me for the job—my good relationship with him had afforded me an opportunity when I needed it the most. It was proof that building and maintain relationships is essential and important.

Lessons Learned

31. Do every job well.

32. Know what your boss has in mind for your future success.

33. Be careful not to miss opportunities to advance.

34. Always be yourself. Do not imitate others.

35. Always stick to your principles, even if this means danger in the short term; play the long game.

36. Take advice from mentors and authority figures; ask questions and listen to their answers.

37. Experience is an investment in the future.

38. Do the right thing; you will be rewarded in the end.

CHAPTER 6

COMMON VALUES, 1968–1971

EXPERIENCE AS AN EDUCATION

Years later at a dinner with the director of the Small Business Administration of Japan, I asked him, "What's important to you?"

His answer summed up the main lesson of my time as international sales director at Sonesta. "My wife, my children, my country," he said.

I would have given the same answer. Regardless of race, age, country of origin, or the other categories by which people define themselves, I can't imagine who wouldn't agree with this answer.

As international sales director—and during the years previous and afterward—my career in business introduced me to a diverse population with as many different types of personalities. Working with people is challenging. It has both helped me to solidify my own values and taught me that, at our core, people value the same things.

At Sonesta, the management hierarchy in the sales department was vice president of marketing at the top, followed by general sales manager, then international sales director—the position I held. I worked for Bob McGrail, who was a very nice man. The job mirrored my earlier position as New York area sales manager: my office was again next to the Plaza, and I had the same responsibilities, except that as international sales director, rather than working with hotels in New York, Boston, and Washington, I was working with hotels in Europe and the Caribbean. The regional sales directors in Europe—Rome, Frankfurt, London, and Paris—reported to me.

I had been prepared for my new position by my extensive and varied previous job experiences. By moving from one job to another and learning the skill set of each, I was building an impressive and comprehensive résumé. My experience prepared me for new challenges. It was like I was walking up a set of stairs, with each new job teaching me the balance and building the muscles I would need to conquer the next.

I was prepared to be international sales director (where I needed to work with several organizations in multiple countries) by learning about administrative and financial tasks as the administrative director of the Practicing Law Institute and gaining experience managing people abroad as the resident manager of the Balmoral Beach Hotel in the Bahamas. I was prepared to manage the operations of a hotel as the resident manager of the Balmoral Beach Hotel by learning about operations during my time as director of sales and catering at the Kenmore Hotel. I was prepared to be director of sales and catering at the Kenmore Hotel by gaining the diverse exposure to leadership and sales that I encountered as regional sales manager of the Hotel Corporation of America. I was prepared to work within a large corporation as regional sales manager by acquiring the basic skills of solving problems and negotiating with people that I learned in that first stepping-stone as sales promotion manager at the Roosevelt Hotel.

It was an intensive, on-the-job course that lasted a decade and provided in-depth and practical training in leadership, management, international and domestic relations, sales, operations, distribution systems, and more. Each

> Many people make the mistake of moving on to the next employment situation too soon.

job or position was a course, and I had to pass the final exam in each by mastering the material and performing well in the job. Often when I did not accept a new position, it was because I had not yet learned all that my current position had to teach me. I wanted to make sure that I passed the exam before I moved on.

Many people make the mistake of moving on to the next employment situation too soon. I talk about this often when I give presentations at universities. My advice to young men and women heading out into the working world is this: Don't leave a job for money; leave a job for experience. You can always earn money later, but the gains you will make by finishing a job (or learning a job) are invaluable, as they are what will allow you to succeed in further experiences. In the early years of a career, people should build a base of experience and knowledge that is transferable and will be used for the entirety of their careers.

HOTEL SALES AND MARKETING ASSOCIATION

Although I had participated as a member in the Hotel Sales Association earlier (now called the Hotel Sales and Marketing Association), I became more active and began to rise in the organization in 1969 when I took the position of international sales director at Sonesta. The Hotel Sales and Marketing Association is an international association of hospitality, marketing, and salespeople with local chapters. People in the industry gather for seminars, leadership groups, and workshops that teach business-related strategies. In addition, it provides a community where people in the hospitality industry can connect, problem solve, and gain a perspective that their work and the industry is larger than their individual jobs. Through the association, members gain self-respect and respect for others in the industry.

When I first joined the Hotel Sales and Marketing Association, it was mainly focused on corporate travel that involved conventions and meetings. It was devoid of anyone knowledgeable about the luxury travel business. In addition, travel agents at that time didn't handle personal or individual business travel outside of resort bookings. I saw an opportunity. I called Bud Grice, the president of the association. "Would you be interested in having someone work for the association who has experience in the travel industry?" I asked him.

As the international sales director, I was able to call on the work I did as the resident manager at the Balmoral Beach Hotel in the Bahamas. I had experience in business dealings with travel agencies and could both offer my expertise and teach others in the association about the luxury travel business. I offered to chair a committee. Grice agreed. I became chairman of a committee focused on the travel industry and a member of the board of directors.

I was promoted over the next years. By 1976, I was president of the association.

Through the Hotel Sales and Marketing Association, I met my peers and became part of a supportive community, learned from the experiences of others, and imparted my own unique knowledge of the hotel and travel industry. As a professional, it is important to be involved with your industry through professional organizations like this and to know that you are a part of a history and community that is bigger than the individual organization for which you work. Connecting with your peers offers opportunities for networking and coop-eration as well as an education and access to invaluable mentorship.

Although I am long retired from the position of president, I continue to be involved with the Hotel Sales and Marketing Association by funding an annual leadership conference. My involvement with the organization also spurred my involvement with and organization of other national associations.

LONDON

When I began the position of international sales director, Sonesta was expanding internationally, especially in Europe. They already owned the Carlton Tower in London and were in the process of building hotels in Milan and Munich. They also had operations in Puerto Rico, Bermuda, and Nassau. Because of this, in addition to my office near the Plaza, I also had sales offices in Frankfurt, Paris, and Rome. I had dealings with the heads of many large institutions, with local governments, with my own salespeople, and with salespeople from other organizations.

For some people, embarking on international business—wherein you conduct business in other countries with people from other cultures and backgrounds—may have been difficult. I found it to be no different from conducting business in the US. My past experience had prepared me to interact with people who held different perspec-tives from my own and in situations with which I was unfamiliar. I was tolerant of others and accustomed to looking for the commonali-ties that people shared. Still, there were experiences that presented unexpected challenges.

The first time I traveled to London, I went to see George Dekorn-feld, who was the manager for all the hotels in Europe operated by Sonesta. I knew him from my years at the Plaza—he had been the assistant to the general manager when I was the marketing director. An employee who worked in marketing picked me up at the airport. As we drove toward Dekornfeld's office in the city, he said to me, "What kind of a date would you like tonight?"

The question caught me off guard. "What do you mean?" I asked.

He explained, "Usually when visiting people come to town, they want a blonde or brunette or something like that."

I was shocked. "I don't want any dates," I told him. I realize now how naive I was then. It was the 1970s, and things like that happened then and were acceptable among a certain crowd. Many CEOs were matched with dates on any and all business trips; however, it was not then, nor was it ever, my way of doing business, and the concept was completely foreign to me.

What I gleaned from that experience was really a two-tiered lesson. The first was that you shouldn't pass judgment on things outside your own domain. Building relationships with people in other countries, in other sectors of business, or in other businesses requires understanding their way of doing things, or at least an effort to understand, and the development of some tolerance for a different way of doing things. It was not my place to impose a judgment on what other people did or what they found acceptable in that situation.

In saying that, however, the second lesson I learned was that one must also decide what behaviors they will tolerate and what they will not; what they can participate in and still maintain their personal values and integrity, and what they must reject. While I felt that it was tolerable to do business with people who found it acceptable to have the hotel find them dates, I could not tolerate engaging in this behavior myself.

Overall, what I believe is that it is the responsibility of a leader to set the example they want others to follow. Leaders set examples both through their own behavior and in the ways they choose to respond to the behaviors of others. Leaders must behave properly. The standards that a person holds themselves to as an individual reflect on individual character, but when representing a business, individual behavior must meet the standards of that business. As a leader in business, you set the example for those standards. That includes the way you behave in complex moral situations but also in daily routines: when you arrive to and leave from work, with what level you commit to tasks, the general attitude with which you approach your work. Employees follow the examples set by leaders, whether they are good or bad.

MUNICH

My first trip to Germany was to Munich in 1972, when I went to meet Sales Director Hans Henrik Van Koller. I had seen films about Munich and heard stories of World War II, but I really did not know what to expect about the city or the country of, what was then, West Germany.

Hans met me at the airport. There was little security then. I deplaned on the tarmac and walked down the stairs to see a man holding a sign with my name on it. Hans was my age—a tall, handsome, quintessential German-looking man with blond hair and blue eyes wearing a trench coat.

Hans was very friendly and spoke perfect English. We spent the first day and a half of my visit in his office going over the sales plan. In the evening we had dinner together and talked about work and also about our families, interests, and upbringings. It was not even thirty years after World War II, and the general perception that people in the US had of Germany was still strongly influenced by the war and the rise of the Nazi Party; however, it was obvious to me that Hans was not a Nazi Party supporter. I looked at him as someone much like me: a young businessman.

On the second day, we finished our business around noon. "Is there anything that you would like to see or do in Munich?" Hans asked.

I told him that I would like to visit Dachau, the World War II concentration camp that sits about forty minutes outside of Munich. I offered to find my own way, but Hans volunteered to drive me.

When we arrived at Dachau, I assumed that Hans was only dropping me off and asked what time I should expect to be picked up.

"I would like to go through it with you," Hans said. "I've never been."

I was taken aback and also a bit hesitant and overly sensitive about walking through Dachau—as a Jew whose father had fought for the US in World War II—with Hans, a German. I didn't understand why he would want to see Dachau, and I also worried that he might feel guilty or uncomfortable being there with me. But we got out of the car and began to walk through the camp together.

Dachau was a concentration camp, not an extermination camp like Auschwitz or Treblinka. When you enter Dachau, you are first shown a film about the rise of the Nazi Party in Germany. Hans and I sat and watched Hitler commanding Nazi troops on a screen. Then we walked through an exhibit displaying uniforms worn by various prisoners according to how they were classified based on race, religion, gender, or sexual preference. Finally we went outside and crossed a courtyard made of stones. We didn't speak, and as we were walking, it was nearly silent, except for the crunch of our feet on the gravel. Across the courtyard were the barracks where hundreds of people were housed in buildings smaller than the upstairs of my house in Atlanta now. Each barrack held a sign announcing how many people it had held. It was unimaginable. Beyond that stood the buildings where they burned the bodies of the dead.

In the middle of the courtyard, there was a sculpture with an inscription in English and German: "Those who cannot remember the past are condemned to repeat it." The quote was taken from a book written by philosopher George Santayana.

"Hans," I said, "George Santayana was a graduate of my high school in Boston in the early twentieth century, and here's his name." That was the only thing we said to each other during the visit.

My anxieties about walking through Dachau with Hans were not justified. He did not seem to feel guilty or wary. He walked through like he was walking through any museum, interested in the history and facts. Of course, it was history. I remembered visiting the Southern Museum of Civil War in Kennesaw, Georgia, where I saw the grave-stones of ten thousand southerners who were killed in the Civil War. As I walked through, I felt mournful, but it was a distant and general sadness.

As Hans drove me back to the city, I asked him if he remembered anything about World War II. I knew that, like me, he must have been only seven or eight during that time.

"I grew up and in the eastern area," he told me. "The Prussian area of Germany. What I remember is my mother putting me under the kitchen table when the American planes were bombing my city."

His memories and perceptions of World War II were so different from my own. I did not tell him about my memories of the war or the associations that I had with Germany and the Nazis and all that the Nazis had done. What I said to him was, "I understand." It taught me that people can have completely different experiences of the same event. Ultimately, you can't assume that people will all have the same associations.

FRANKFURT

Later, in Frankfurt during a business trip, I found myself in the apartment of Bernt Brings, the sales manager of the Frankfurt office. Bernt was a wonderful and very worldly man who spoke perfect English. He had a small two-bedroom apartment in the city where he and his wife had transformed the second bedroom into a library. While he was busy preparing coffee, he left me in his library to look around.

I examined the books on the shelves, most of which were written in German, reading the titles. My heart stopped when I came across *Mein Kampf*. I took it from the shelf and held it. I opened the cover and read the scrolling inscription in pen: "Zu Herr Brings"—To Mr. Brings. I couldn't believe it. Beneath it, in looping handwriting was the signature: Adolph Hitler. My hands trembled.

Bernt came into the room behind me and I turned to look at him.

"Where did you get this?" I asked.

"My father was a mayor in a small town in Bavaria, and Hitler came through when he was running for office in 1933," Bernt explained casually. "He was giving out autographed copies of his book." When Bernt's father died, the book was passed to Bernt and found its way to the shelf in his library.

I put the book back on the shelf, still feeling the weight of it in my hands. I couldn't believe that I had held something once touched by Adolph Hitler. If that book had come into my possession, I would have gotten rid of it—sold it or donated it to a museum; I would not have wanted it in my home. For me, the book and the signature signified something greater than the pages—the horrors and evils of the Third Reich.

However, what was clear to me then was that Bernt's perspective differed from my own, and his associations with the book and autograph were personal and unique to his own experience—a memory of his father. I imagined Bernt as a child looking up to his father, who was the mayor of a small town; I imagined an important political figure coming through town and honoring his father as mayor; I imagined how proud this must have made Bernt. When Bernt thought of that book, he did not think of the words within it—as I did—and the way they had helped to change an ideology and allow for the persecution, imprisonment, and murder of so many people; he did not think of the signature as belonging to the orchestrator of those many cruelties. He saw that book and the signature as a gesture of recognition for his father, the leader of the small town where he had grown up. I could not judge him for keeping and valuing the book.

AN INTERNATIONAL PERSPECTIVE

There are situations for which there is no training. I could not have been prepared to hold *Mein Kampf* in my hands, nor to tour Dachau with a man who had been bombed by American troops during World War II, nor to have to politely refuse the offer to be set up on a date. I was able to negotiate these situations and build relationships with people internationally because of the mindset I held and the value system that I maintained. I had a job that entailed working with local management to improve their sales and marketing. I went to these other countries with the aim of using my expertise in the business to help them develop strategies that would work for them. I did not believe that I was superior to them but instead found that our business goals were in line with one another and that our personal values were the same.

My modus operandi as a manager and leader did not change when I worked in other countries. My focus and interest was still on the human side of the business. Sometimes people in managerial positions make the mistake of going overseas to the sales offices in Munich, London, or Milan and, as the leader, proclaiming, "This is the way we do things in New York, so you've got things the same here." Instead, I went to other countries with a desire to learn and understand, a reverence for differences, and a goal to treat every person with the same respect with which I had always treated American people. The key is not to demand that other people conform to your way of doing things but to build a relationship, understand the workings of the other place, and then decide what needs to be done to guarantee success. True success requires this kind of flexibility that allows for unique business strategies appropriate to each individual situation.

> The secret of success really is in the human side of the enterprise.

When conducting business internationally, or domestically for that matter, the key is not to focus on the differences between people but to notice the similarities and shared values. Even when working in countries that operate under very different political systems, or within different cultures, even when laws and regulations differ greatly, or different technologies are being used, I have found that people's personal concerns are very much the same. People often ask me how I am able to communicate so effectively and conduct business so successfully internationally. The secret of success really is in the human side of the enterprise. As much as people may come from different histories, political systems, cultures, and backgrounds, at our root, we are very much the same.

Lessons Learned

39. International work is not a mystery. You share common values with all people no matter their country of residence or origin.

40. As a leader, you set an example for others with your behavior. They will follow.

41. Understand where people are coming from before you make a decision that affects them. Be aware that their perception of situations may differ from your own.

42. Whatever the system of government or economics that people live under, people behave based on similar values. Leadership, by government and institutions, is what allows people to act effectively and well.

CHAPTER 7

A PASS, AN ELIMINATION, AND AN ACHIEVEMENT, 1972–1974

MANAGING UP, MANAGING DOWN

As with the situation in the Bahamas, I continued to be overlooked by my bosses for promotions and opportunities. One day I became frustrated and said to Jim Lavenson, a mentor whom I'd met during my years in business, "I don't understand. Why am I having trouble?"

"You're very good at managing down," he told me, "but you're terrible at managing up."

"I thought the job was managing down," I said.

"No, that's not the only job," Jim said. "You also have to manage up."

It was career-changing advice.

Some people are very good at managing up the line, and some people are very good at managing down the line. But if you want to be successful in the corporate world (or any world), you've got to be concerned about managing both ways.

Managing down means being concerned with and paying attention to the people who work for you. I was always good at this and took great care to mentor, teach, guide, and lead those who were in my charge. Managing up means being concerned with and paying attention to the people for whom you work. This I did not entirely understand in my early years in management. As a salesman, when the boss told me to go out and make sales calls, I followed this instruction, but I did not consider why my boss wanted me to make particular calls, what he hoped I would achieve, or how this would affect his job. Because I was not really considering his business goals and needs, I did not communicate as effectively as I could have. It was natural for me to spend my time helping those who were under my management, but I didn't realize that I needed to take the same time to help those who were managing me.

Managing up means taking the time to listen to and understand the larger agenda of the people above you and the company as a whole. As I continued in my career and became adept at managing up, people wanted to hire me because they saw that I was working to achieve the goals of the company and never put my agenda before the agenda of the people for whom I worked. After Jim pointed out my shortcoming, I worked on listening to my bosses, understanding what they wanted from me, and executing their strategies accordingly. Because I understood what they wanted, I was able to report to them more effectively.

Later, I met a lot of managers and saw many people who were not promoted because they had the opposite problem to the one I'd had: they were good at managing up and terrible at managing down. They got along well with their bosses and understood the goals and agenda of the company, but they didn't work well with the employees in their charge. A successful manager and leader finds a way to balance and focus on both managing up and managing down.

BACK TO BOSTON

In 1970, I learned that Sonesta's vice president of marketing was leaving the company. Bob McGrail was being promoted into the position, and he wanted to promote me to general sales manager, where I would again be based at the Sonesta headquarters in Boston. My third son had just been born. Andrea and I sold our house in New Jersey, bought a new house in Sudbury, Massachusetts, and moved with our three sons—now five, three, and a few months old—back to the Boston area. By then, my father had married the woman who he'd been dating. Sadly, she was nothing like my mother and I didn't get along with her.

It was in Sudbury that my children really began their childhoods. They became involved in ice hockey and other activities. People often ask me how I balanced my personal and business life given the time demands of many of the professional positions that I've held. It is very possible to be a successful corporate leader, a successful businessperson, a successful father, and successful husband. You must budget time for each and give each your full attention to every present moment. I would purposefully schedule meetings before or after games so that I could be there to cheer on my sons; I would come home for lunch; when I needed to make business trips, I would be gone for the least amount of time possible, sometimes making a round trip in a single day. I wanted to be involved in my family life. It was an important part of the way that I planned my business endeavors. My family, especially Andrea, also always had a major role in my career. Andrea never resented that my work meant that we had to relocate several times. She was always included in such decisions and influenced the choices that shaped my career.

I did not find a replacement to fill my old position as international sales director. Instead, I undertook both positions, managing the sales of all the Sonesta hotels in the United States as general sales manager and managing sales and marketing abroad as the international sales manager. It was a big but manageable job, and in the following years, it became much smaller.

In 1972, the Sonesta Corporation found itself in financial trouble. Sonesta had taken out a loan from a German bank, and the US dollar was losing value against the Deutschmark, making it difficult to make payments on the loan. They sold their hotels in Munich and Milan to Hilton. The only hotel they kept in Europe was the Carlton Tower Hotel in London.

Then I got a call from Joe McCarthy, who had been the sales director at the Roosevelt when I'd worked there. He was now the national sales vice president for the Sheraton Corporation, which was a top-level job at a very well-established organization. He wanted to hire me as the northeast sales director for Sheraton.

Sheraton was a much larger company than Sonesta with far more holdings, and the position would have entailed a lot more responsibility. I went to see McCarthy in the Sheraton building in Boston. After listening to his offer, I told him, "No thanks." McGrail, my current boss and the vice president of marketing, was a great guy, and Sonesta had been good to me. I was happy where I was, even though the offer was more money and more prestige.

A month later, McGrail called me into his office. "Mike, I'm leaving," he said. "I've taken a position as the northeast sales director for Sheraton."

"Congratulations," I said. I didn't tell McGrail that McCarthy had offered me the job first.

Shortly thereafter, the president of the Sonesta Company and McGrail's boss, Paul Sonnabend, called me. I had known Sonnabend for years. I was away on business and staying at the Admiral Benbow Inn in Memphis, Tennessee, at the time. I expected that he would officially announce that McGrail had resigned and offer me the position. Instead, after informing me that McGrail had vacated his position, he told me that he was going to replace McGrail with the general manager of one of the hotels in Washington, DC. I was crushed. Someone had taken my place. It felt like the Bahamas all over again. I had previous marketing experience from the Plaza, and I knew the offices and operations in Boston inside and out, but Sonnabend wanted to bring in someone with no experience who was unfamiliar with the situation.

I was distraught. I called Andrea and told her everything. "McGrail took the job that I turned down, and I'm not getting the marketing job." The general manager from DC didn't know anything about marketing. "I can't believe this is happening," I said. I broke down.

"You've got to come home," Andrea said. "Come back to Boston. Go see Sonnabend, and tell him you want the vice president of marketing job. You deserve it. Tell him that you turned down the job that McGrail took."

I flew home the following day, walked into Sonnabend's office, and said, "Paul, you can't do this to me. It's not right for the company. It's not right for me. It's unfair. The person you selected is a general manager who doesn't know about marketing or sales. I know the people. I know the job." Then I added, "By the way, I turned down the Sheraton job to stay here."

Sonnabend agreed. In 1972, he made me Sonesta's vice president of marketing. I had very nearly not received the promotion that I had earned, one in which I knew I could do well. I couldn't put it into words yet, but I was having difficulties managing up. Sonnabend had not noticed or thought of me because I had forgotten to truly include him in my considerations. My wife was right to urge me to act.

DUNFEY

In 1973, Sonesta was in financial trouble. The company informed me that they were going to reduce staff and eliminate the vice president of marketing position—my job. They offered me options: I could be the general manager of their hotel in Bermuda or the director of marketing at the Plaza. I knew that I didn't want to move my young children to Bermuda, and the position at the Plaza seemed like a step backward. Neither option seemed correct for me at the time.

My sales promotion manager then was a woman named Barbara Borin. Borin was dating (and would later marry) Walter Dunfey of the Dunfey Brothers, a company that owned hotels in New Hampshire. The life insurance company, Aetna, had just purchased Dunfey, and Dunfey was expanding.

Shortly after I was told that Sonesta was eliminating my position, Borin walked into my office and said, "Walter Dunfey would like to talk to you about becoming vice president of marketing for Dunfey Hotels."

Aetna had recently purchased the Dunfey Hotel Company. They were in the process of rehabilitating the Parker House Hotel in Boston, the oldest continually operating hotel in the United States, established in 1840. Aetna had given Dunfey funds to upgrade the Parker House Hotel facilities, and they were looking for people who knew how to handle upscale properties. In addition to the Parker House Hotel, they also owned some motels and a couple of other upscale properties like Parker House. They also acquired the Royal Coaches in Houston,

Dallas, San Mateo, and Atlanta, which were mainly meeting and conference facilities. Because Aetna had not previously been in the hotel business, and Dunfey had not owned so many properties in the past, the company did not know how to use or market those properties. They were looking for guidance.

Part of the process for getting hired at Dunfey was to interview with a psychologist named Dr. Fred Jervis, who consulted for them. Jervis's job was to evaluate potential executives to see how they would fit with the company.

I arrived at the interview to discover that Dr. Jervis was blind—something no one at Dunfey had mentioned. Because Dr. Jervis was blind, he did not judge people based on what they were wearing or their physical appearance; he assessed people based entirely on what they said. In other words, it was impossible to positively or negatively impress Dr. Jervis because one wore an expensive tie or a well-fitting suit. We had a conversation, and solely based on what I told him and how I told him those things, he made a judgment about my personality. We had a wonderful conversation, and I was entirely fascinated by him and his methods. We became great friends.

I later learned that Dr. Jervis had his own management system: the back-planning system. It was based on his philosophical belief that you create your own change based on your own goals.

"That's how you make changes," he explained to me. "Most people react to things that happen. But with the back-planning system, you don't wait for things to happen. You identify what results you want, decide what you have to do to secure those results, then act to make changes to get those results. You measure your strategies along the way."

The system is used widely now and not only intended for use in business but also in personal life. Dr. Jervis had his own company called the Center for Constructive Change, which taught other organizations how to apply the back-planning system. I learned the system and continued to use it as a management strategy for the next decades as I moved from one company to the next. I also continued to hire Dr. Jervis as a consultant to help me teach the system until he died.

Months after Walter Dunfey sent me to talk to Dr. Jervis, I went to work for the Dunfey Company. It was March 1973. Shortly after I left, Sonesta sold the Plaza, along with other hotels, and became a much smaller company.

Working for Dunfey as the vice president of marketing was a major change. I reported to Patrick (Pat) Henry Ford, the executive vice president of operations. Ford had been working for the Dunfey family for decades. He'd started in a lower-level position and worked his way up. In the next years, he taught me more about hotel operations than I had learned in all my previous years. He taught me how to plan budgets, how to run budget meetings with the general managers, how to review the P&Ls every month, and how to do all the foundational and basic tasks of running a business in great detail. While I had been involved in related duties at Sonesta, no one really ever taught me the practical ins and outs of management in that way. I went to hotel after hotel with Pat Ford, preparing for and helping to conduct meetings.

Together, Jervis and Ford made an enormous impact on my professional life. Twelve years at Sonesta combined with more years at the Practicing Law Institute hadn't taught me all I needed to know. Jervis and Ford showed me how to affect my future and the future of a company.

CHANGE THE OUTCOME

The Dunfey family recognized in me the ability to effect change. My experiences up until then, along with the lessons I learned from Dr.

Fred Jervis and Pat Ford, gave me a toolbox of strategies for managing people. I didn't need to be an expert on everything—economics, new technologies, other cultures—I just had to concentrate on how to get the desired results by finding the right people to do the jobs and motivating them appropriately. Every situation requires a different approach, but my overall philosophical strategy was aimed at changing the outcome. That is what the Dunfey family saw in me and what companies continued to see in me throughout my career. Nobody hires you to maintain the status quo; they hire you to be different, to be innovative, and to make change.

Before I was hired, the Dunfey family purchased the Parker House. It was viewed as an old relic by Boston's hotel market. It had been rehabilitated three times previously by other hotel companies. None of the rehabilitations had helped the hotel to be successful. The Dunfey family changed the name of the hotel to the Dunfey Parker House and charged me and Regional Vice President Ed Chekijian with making the hotel profitable.

The previous rehabilitations, and the current one enacted by Dunfey, all involved major restoration of the physical structure. Dunfey redesigned the rooms and built a club downstairs, along with an elegant dining room. Ed Chekijian and I were responsible for devising and facilitating a marketing plan.

The first change we made was to the uniforms of the hotel employees. The Parker House Hotel is located in the heart of Boston, across the street from the Old Granary Burial Ground (where three signers of the Declaration of Independence are buried) and from the final resting place of Benjamin Franklin's father. It is also near the original site of the Boston Latin School. The hotel itself is very historic and is surrounded by the historic district of the city and along the famous Freedom Trail. We needed to capitalize on the tourist structure already in place that was focused on historical Boston. We put the doorman, housekeepers, bellmen, and other employees in colonial-style uniforms that fit the theme of the location. This alone began to transform the hotel into a theatrical site.

I knew that the challenge was twofold: a unique campaign personalized for the goals and challenges of the hotel had not been devised, and the plan needed to be properly executed. We needed both the right plan and the follow-through to put the plan into action (strategies that the previous companies who had bought Parker House had failed to implement). Chekijian and I then met with Hill Holliday, a major advertising firm in Boston, to discuss advertising campaign possibilities. A man named Jack Connors was the president of Hill Holiday at the time.

"Look," I said to Connors, "this hotel has been rehabilitated and remarketed three times, and it failed each time. When we go to market with this hotel, nobody's going to believe that it could be a success. Your challenge is to come up with a plan to change the minds of people who expect to be disappointed."

A couple of weeks later, Connors and Hill Holliday proposed a campaign called Dunfey's Parker House, the Goodnight Guarantee. "The Goodnight Guarantee is very simple," Connors told me. "You don't like it, you don't pay for it. Period."

I looked at Chekijian. Then I looked at Ford, who was my boss. Then I said, "I think that's great. Let's do it."

Somebody in the meeting asked, "What's going to happen if somebody just walks up to the front desk and says, 'I didn't like my stay'?"

"We'll tell him, 'That's fine, sir. Don't pay for it,'" I confirmed.

It was an aggressive stance. No one had ever offered such a guarantee in the hotel business. But I knew that for Parker House to regain credibility in the market, we would need to guarantee that we could perform; we had to build trust with the customers and reestablish the hotel's reputation based on that service.

Our new Goodnight Guarantee garnered us tremendous publicity in the *Boston Globe* and other publications. The marketing team dedicated itself to the historic theme and created a menu for the restaurant that focused on traditional New England foods. We also continued to make bold and innovative moves at Dunfey Parker House Hotel. For example, we were the first major American hotel to feature Californian, rather than European, wines, offering Mondavi cabernet and chardonnay as our pouring wines.

Connors was surprised that we accepted his Goodnight Guarantee. Often when an outside contractor presents an idea, even a great one, they have trouble convincing a traditional company to set aside objections from legal, accounting, and other departments to employ the new strategy. Establishments with legacy systems are generally afraid to make dramatic changes. I had been able to advocate for the creative suggestions offered by Connors and Hill Holliday, and I was fortunate that the Dunfey family trusted my judgment. Dunfey was ready and willing to make groundbreaking moves. It worked very well. The successful rehabilitation of Dunfey Parker House Hotel gave Dunfey a broader reputation and an opportunity to grow.

Ford was very pleased. He and I are still good friends these many years later. Recently he was being honored with a lifetime achievement award, and he asked if I would fly to Phoenix to present the award to him. I was privileged to do so. In my speech, I acknowledged all that Pat had done for me and what he'd done for the business. A significant amount of my success is based on the foundation and opportunities he gave me. After I returned home, he sent me a gift that I still have sitting in my bar in Florida: a twenty-year-old bottle of port wine in a box with an inscription that reads, "God's greatest gift is good friends." In my lifetime, I have found that to be profoundly true.

WINS AND LOSSES

In 1974, Chekijian left Dunfey. I had been with the company for a year and a half, and Ford asked me what I really wanted to do within Dunfey. I said, "I want to be supervisor of operations." He thought I was ready and promoted me to regional vice president of operations in charge of Dunfey Parker House Hotel, the Hyannis Resort, and the four Royal Coaches in San Mateo, Houston, Dallas, and Atlanta. They were the biggest properties in the company. Ford was certain that my ability to think creatively and take innovative and courageous direction would benefit the company.

It was the first time that I was responsible for hiring general managers, and I was excited to do so. As a person in sales, general managers had always been a thorn in my side; they often simply didn't understand sales. Most of them came from backgrounds in the food and beverage or finance industries. I was going to make a change. I promoted the sales director of the Hyannis to be general manager; I hired Gunther Hatt, who I'd worked with at Sonesta, to manage the Royal Coaches in Houston; and I promoted another Dunfey employ to be general manager of the Dallas property. I chose people with whom I had worked well in the past, whom I liked, and whom I knew could get the jobs done well.

When I became regional vice president of operations, the four Royal Coaches were already struggling. The one in Dallas was located near the Love Field airport and actually faring pretty well. It held six hundred rooms and was running at about 80 percent occupancy. Then, in 1974, the Dallas-Fort Worth International Airport was built west of Dallas, and Love Field was closed. Overnight, our occupancy went from 80 percent to 6 percent. We had to find a new source of business for the hotel. We set up a big sales operation and started to turn the hotel around; however, it never returned to 80 percent occupancy. One night I got a phone call from Joe DePalma, the general manager in Dallas. One of the buildings was on fire. It was completely unoccupied and had been since the airport closed.

"Did you call the fire department?" I asked the manager.

"No," he said, "I called you."

"How bad is it?" I asked.

"It's going to go," he said.

It was a blessing in disguise. Even with all the efforts I'd made to market the hotel, the occupancy numbers were still down. I knew that it couldn't recover completely with the loss of the airport traffic. "Make sure it goes," I said, knowing that the building burning down was actually a blessing. "But call the fire department."

After the fire, Dunfey rebuilt the structure but transformed it into a training facility for Braniff Airways crews. The new building housed an airplane simulator and an entire plane where the airline held instruction for flight attendants.

In the following months, I was also able to make the other three Royal Coaches profitable, although none of their transformations were as dramatic as the one in Dallas.

As regional vice president of operations, I also developed destiny accounts. Destiny accounts were large accounts that booked multiple or permanent rooms—often accounts belonging to airline crews or major corporations. These were single accounts that brought in a lot of revenue. Acquiring these could really move the needle on our profit margins. I promoted the Dunfey Parker House sales director, Gerald DePietro, to sales director for all the Dunfey hotels, and together we targeted sales to destiny accounts, deciding to which corporations we could sell our hotels and creating a focused marketing campaign as opposed to the broad sales effort that had been in place earlier. Our new strategy simplified sales. We were now considering 10 rather than 150 accounts. Our efforts were more effective, and the campaign guaranteed profit improvement.

EMPLOYEE REVIEWS

At Dunfey, I was given the opportunity to think outside the box. I applied creative and innovative strategies that broke from traditional ideas of sales and management and that ultimately wielded success for the company. But while Dunfey as a company was often willing to try new strategies, they were still hindered by old practices that had been in place for decades without consideration. One of those practices was the annual employee salary review.

Through Dunfey's employee review system, employees in senior positions, like me, met with Jack Dunfey, the president of the company, once a year and talked about their previous year's progress. They were then given raises based on Dunfey's assessment of their performances. At the end of my first year at Dunfey, I sat outside Jack Dunfey's office waiting for my review. Paul McGown, the head of purchasing, was also waiting. McGown had worked at Dunfey for twenty-five years.

"What can you tell me about these reviews?" I asked McGown.

"You don't have to worry," McGown told me. "I don't participate in these fancy reviews. I just go in and say, 'Jack, just tell me the number and I'll leave.'"

It was a riot, but it also presented an interesting point. Although it is standard for large companies to hold annual salary reviews, I've never been a big believer in them. As a manager, you should be reviewing your employees on a consistent basis, not just at the end of the year. The annual system was ineffective and antiquated. Many years later, when I was running the aquarium in Atlanta, I got rid of the review system entirely. It only generated more work hours for human resources; the reviews themselves elicited no helpful information. As a manager, you should be reviewing your direct reports quarterly, at minimum, and providing employees with constructive evaluations, not just an annual review.

After a long wait outside the office, it was finally my turn to talk to Dunfey. I sat across from him for twenty minutes and engaged in a polite conversation about nothing. McGown had been right; the best thing to do would have been to say to Dunfey, "Hit me with a number" and then leave. The afternoon was a waste of my time and his. It was a waste of the company's resources. It took the responsibility of the review away from my immediate supervisor, Pat Ford—someone in a better position to offer real assessment and advice related to my job performance. I was already thinking then about the ways that I could do things differently when I was in charge of a company.

Lessons Learned

43. An offer from another company or organization may look better, but often staying in place can be the right decision, even if your current position offers less compensation.

44. Sometimes you have to be aggressive when going after a position that you really deserve. Go for it.

45. Notice how often relationships with peers, subordinates, and bosses can influence your life.

46. Be on the lookout for other ways of working. You can always learn a better way.

47. Focus on results and plan your desired goals, working backward from your starting position.

48. If you want to change the outcome, invoke new strategies.

49. As a manager or leader, provide your employees with consistent evaluations and conversations about their performance. Do not do this only once a year.

CHAPTER 8

THE SKY'S THE LIMIT, 1975–1985

ANOTHER CHANGE IN DIRECTION

In 1974, a couple of major events changed my life. The first was that my father had a debilitating stroke that left him unable to speak. After the stroke, he came to visit us one weekend. His second wife called me and asked, "Is your father there?"

"Yes," I said. "Do you want me to bring him home?"

"No," she said. "You keep him." She was kicking him out of the house.

As usual, I was traveling a lot, and I had to leave shortly thereafter for a business trip. I asked Andrea if she would look for a residential facility for my father. I didn't think we could take care of him—I was away a lot, the majority of the burden would fall to Andrea, we didn't have very much money, and we had three little kids to look after.

When I came home, Andrea told me that she'd toured three facilities. "I wouldn't put my father in any of them," she told me, "and I'm not putting your father in them either."

My father moved in with us and ended up living with Andrea, me, and our three small children for the next six years.

That same year, Aetna decided to sell Dunfey to Aer Lingus, an Irish airline, that wanted to expand their holdings to include hotels in the United States. As they were in the process of negotiations, I got a job offer through a headhunter to become the senior vice president of marketing of Americana Hotels, a company owned by American Airlines and based in New York City.

I went to interview with the CEO of American Airlines, Al Casey. I'd never met with the CEO of such an enormous company like that in my life. At the end of the interview, Casey asked if I had any questions. I said, "Yes, sir. How do you run a billion-dollar company like this?"

"I don't run it," he said. "My people run it. I manage the board. I work on the big strategies, but my people run the company."

His response really stayed with me. Casey was not trying to do it all. He understood that the job was too big for any one person. He hired people whom he trusted to manage day-to-day operations and marketing for his firm, and they in turn hired people whom they trusted to work with other staff and customers. Because Casey allowed other people to do their jobs and take care of the details, he was free to work on the overall picture.

At that time I was making $44,000 a year at Dunfey; Americana Hotels offered me $70,000 with stock options, a pension plan, and an American Airlines Positive Space Pass—free first-class tickets to fly anywhere, anytime for my family and me.

Jack Dunfey wanted me to stay with Dunfey. He offered to give me a raise to $55,000 a year and a bigger car: an Oldsmobile in place of my Chevrolet. He also offered to make me executive vice president of operations.

"That's Pat Ford's job," I said.

He said, "Pat Ford can work for you."

I went home and talked to Andrea about the two offers.

There were two major problems with staying at Dunfey. One was that the new position would mean that Andrea and I would have to move our family to New Hampshire, a place where Andrea didn't especially want to live. The second was that, after all that he'd done for me, I didn't want to disrespect Ford by taking his position. The job with Americana Hotels was a move back to marketing and sales, and while I really wanted to be in operations, it seemed the better choice.

I took the job with Americana Hotels in 1975, and Andrea and I moved our children and my father to Stamford, Connecticut. American Airlines was a billion-dollar company, and it was a big move for me, akin to being transferred from the minor to the major leagues. It would prove to be a much bigger job than any I had held previously, where I would be responsible for marketing larger hotels and more of them—including properties in Hawaii, Samoa, Korea, Mexico, Bal Harbor, New York City, and Washington, DC. In addition, Americana Hotels was losing money, and American Airlines was not happy about the loss. It was my challenge to make the business profitable. Now I had experience in operations and in sales and marketing, which gave me a broader perspective and more comprehensive skills for addressing the complicated tasks before me.

AMERICANA HOTELS

I took the job as senior vice president of marketing for Americana Hotels in 1976, when my sons were six, eight, and ten years old. The job started in the middle of the school year, and so Andrea stayed with them—and my father—in Boston for six months while they finished the year, and I lived at the Americana Hotel in New York, commuting home to Boston on weekends.

Although Americana Hotels was owned by American Airlines, our marketing and operations were completely separate. Americana Hotels had properties around the country and in many places around the world, including Asia and Central America.

When Machiavelli wrote about governing countries, he suggested that leaders should decide what they needed to do to rule in those new lands effectively, then decide who they could trust to help apply their new strategy and replace those who they could not trust. In other words, a new leader should not go into a company, fire everyone, and hire all new people. Instead, you must assess what is working and not working, decide what must be done to make the company successful, learn which employees will be able to do their jobs well and teach them, and get rid of employees who cannot or will not work to benefit the company.

In many ways, choosing and working with employees is akin to coaching and forming a group of players who can work as a winning team. As someone who had played team sports a great deal in my youth, I understood that I could not make a company successful on my own. I would need a strong team who I could coach to achieve the best results, much like Al Casey. Part of my job was to find the right people.

I needed to make strategic changes, but I also needed to change the entire mentality of the company. I got rid of people who proved themselves to be uncoachable—stuck in traditional ways of doing business and unwilling to be part of the new team—and recruited others. I was fortunate to have worked with many incredible people in the hotel industry before I came to Americana Hotels. I recruited people who I had worked with previously and seen in action, including Michael Kay, who I had been with at Sonesta, to be the new senior vice president of operations; someone I had worked with at Dunfey to manage the hotels in Hawaii; and another Sonesta coworker to manage the properties in Mexico. In some ways, when Americana Hotels hired me, they not only got me but also a select group of people who were willing to come with me. I was a package deal.

The other integral part of my strategy was to coach my team by teaching them, helping them to work together, and giving them a winning strategy. This meant seeing individual strengths and challenges. Some people who were not successful given one model of work could be invaluable if taught a different way of working. As a coach, you want to get the best out of your players. In a work environment, this means helping each employee work to their potential by teaching them necessary skills, supporting their efforts, and giving them the space to express their individual talents.

As a part of teaching new strategies, I introduced Kay to Jervis's back-planning system. He was immediately on board with implementing the strategy widely in the company, and together we used this system to transform the company over the next five years. We began by conducting seminars at Americana Hotels across the country and introducing the back-planning system to the local management. Within five years, we made the company successful and profitable.

YOU CAN'T SAVE IT ALL

During my first year with Americana Hotels, I went with Kay to Puerto Rico to meet with the managers of the Americana Hotel property there. The property was losing a lot of money. We listened to the local management and assessed the situation. The losses were staggering. The property included a casino. For a long time, the casino had been supporting the hotel, but now even the casino was losing money. At that time, the labor costs in Puerto Rico were high, increasing the operating budget significantly. It meant that profit margins for properties in Puerto Rico were generally low. Kay, the local managers, and I concluded that any effort we exerted to make the property successful would cost more than it returned in profits. Sometimes in business

> Sometimes in business you need to know when to cut your losses and get out.

you need to know when to cut your losses and get out. I knew that we needed to close the Americana Hotel in Puerto Rico.

The situation was complicated because the hotel employees belonged to a union. Along with the local management, we were worried that the union could potentially become violent if they learned that Americana Hotels was closing the establishment. We executed a well-planned operation in the middle of the night. We secured rooms for all the current guests at another hotel, and at four o'clock in the morning, we began knocking on the doors of occupied rooms and moving guests to the other hotel. When the guests were safely out of the hotel, we announced to the employees that we were closing the business. It was a tense night and a delicate situation.

Early the next morning, I appeared on a Puerto Rican news show. I didn't speak any Spanish. The interviewer's questions and my answers had to be translated for the audience. I explained to the public that maintaining the hotel and casino was no longer a viable option for Americana Hotels. Later, Americana Hotels sold the hotel and the casino to another company, which lessened Americana's overall loss.

DALLAS

In my five years as senior vice president of marketing for Americana Hotels, we made the struggling company profitable, and American Airlines decided to sell it. The main buyer was Hal Milner, the CEO for

Pick Hotels headquartered in Chicago. Pick Hotels was owned by the Bass Brothers, a private equity company based in Fort Worth, Texas.

In 1980, during the sale of Americana Hotels, American Airlines was also in the process of moving the company headquarters from New York to Dallas. One day I got a call from Bob Crandall, the heir apparent to the CEO of American Airlines, Al Casey.

"We'd like you to come to Dallas," Crandall told me. "I want you to be vice president of sales and advertising for American Airlines," he said.

It was a serious offer for a big job: American Airlines had over ninety salespeople and a big advertising budget.

"Why me?" I asked. I had no experience in the airline industry.

"I've been watching your work with Americana Hotels. I think you'd fit in. I think you'd be good," he said. He mentioned an initiative that I had put in place to deal with customer complaints at Americana Hotels. Because American Airlines was the parent company to Americana Hotels, customer complaints about the hotels went to the airline—something the administration of the airline didn't appreciate. I had created comment cards at the individual hotels—something that many businesses have now but that were unheard of then. It empowered customers to more easily give feedback about their stay and allowed the hotels to deal with issues locally. The new system was very successful.

It occurred to me that, beyond a few actions like the comment cards, Crandall really didn't know anything about what I did. He was making a decision to hire me based entirely on my reputation.

I took a few days to think about Crandall's offer and then called him back. "I don't want to leave the hotel business," I told him.

We parted as friends. I never had regrets about deciding to stay in the hotel business at that point in my career.

After turning down Crandall's offer, I went back on the job market. I got another call, this time from my old boss at the Roosevelt Hotel, Joe McCarthy. He was starting a company in Dallas and wanted hire me as the vice president of operations. Fate seemed to be pulling me toward Dallas.

Andrea and I decided that we should take a look at Dallas. We flew down with our sons, who were then fourteen, twelve, and ten and very involved in athletics. We not only needed to look at schools in the area but also at hockey programs. We put a down payment on a house in Plano, Texas.

Then I called McCarthy and said, "Joe, what are you doing about my moving expenses and my real estate fee?"

"You have to pay those yourself," he said.

In all the other offers I'd been given for jobs over the years, the companies had always provided compensation for relocation. It seemed odd that McCarthy could not offer the same, and it was a sign of how the company might treat me going forward.

"I can't take the job," I told McCarthy.

I decided to keep looking until I found something that would be a better fit for me.

CHICAGO

I got a third call, this time from Hal Milner. "Come to Chicago and be my number two," he said. He offered me the position of executive vice president of operations.

It was a big job and a big move. My father was still living with us, and my middle son's bar mitzvah was scheduled for that following

January. Andrea and I decided that I would go to Chicago alone while my children finished the school year.

In Chicago, Andrea and I needed to find a house large enough to accommodate my children and my father, who was set to move with us. We wanted to live on the North Shore, where the schools had the best reputation. We worked with a real estate broker who took us on a tour of suburbs in the area. I liked a town called Kenilworth.

"I don't think you'd feel comfortable there," the broker told us. It was 1981, but there were still areas where Jewish people couldn't buy a house.

We eventually found a house large enough for our entire family, including my father. Although my dad never fully recovered from his stroke, he was doing well in Stamford. He could get around to some degree, but he had lost most of his ability to speak. We had found a synagogue where he attended a daily senior program. As part of the program, the synagogue picked him up in the mornings and brought him home in the afternoons.

One afternoon, he did not return home. He had met a woman in the program and had gone to visit her. She was a widow.

When I told him that we were moving to Chicago, he shook his head. He did not want to leave Stamford. He had fallen in love with the widow, and I was happy for him.

They were married shortly thereafter and stayed together for the next fifteen years, until my father died. His new wife was a wonderful and kind woman, and they were very happy together.

I moved to the house in the Chicago suburbs that was bigger and more expensive than we now needed. After a year of living in Chicago on my own and commuting home, my family joined me in the house. It was 1981. My sons were fifteen, thirteen, and eleven. They thrived during the next years.

NUMBER TWO

Pick Hotels kept the name Americana Hotels. As executive vice president of operations, I was in charge of everything except finance. I was responsible for all the marketing and operations. In addition to the hotels purchased from Americana Hotels, Pick also had their own hotels, which I oversaw.

Milner was not always easy to work for. He was oriented toward numbers and the financial bottom line rather than focused on people and relationships. That aspect of his personality manifested in different ways. One was that he was not generous when it came to taking care of his employees—there were no bonus programs, no pension programs, and no incentives. His personality also made him very difficult to negotiate with and he was often inflexible, but he was really a decent man and we still remain friends to this day. Years later, in Las Vegas, Hal asked me to give a talk to some people he was working with at the time, which I did. After that, he said to me that there were two hotel people he respected the most. One was Bill Marriott and the second was myself. I was humbled by the statement.

Many people found it difficult to get along with Hal Milner, including Hal Milner's boss at Bass Brothers, Richard Rainwater. In 1984, David Marshall, one of the operating partners working out of Philadelphia, was starting a new hotel company. He called and offered me the position of president and a percentage of ownership of his new company. It meant another move for my family, this time to Philadelphia from Chicago.

I was in the process of accepting the position when I got a call from Rainwater. Marshall and Rainwater partnered on other deals, and when Marshall told Rainwater that I was coming to work for him in Philadelphia, Rainwater told Marshall that he couldn't take me.

Rainwater made an agreement with Milner that Milner would leave the company and I would take Milner's position as president of Americana Hotels.

Managerial and leadership jobs are multifaceted. Companies are ultimately concerned with being profitable, but it is the people who work within those companies who develop the successes—large and small—that create profit.

Lessons Learned

50. When deciding to take or reject a new opportunity that may involve a spouse or family, the decision is not yours alone.

51. Honor those who treat you well both from above and from below.

52. As the Kenny Rogers song says, "You've got to know when hold 'em. Know when to fold 'em." Turning down an opportunity can be as important as accepting one.

53. Always try to leave with the goodwill and friendship you've built (with people and organizations) intact.

PART III

THE DEFINITION OF
SUCCESS

CHAPTER 9

EXPERIENCE AND PRINCIPLES, 1985–1989

ALWAYS TREAT PEOPLE WELL

There are always bumps in the road. Things happen along the way that you cannot control, or you make a mistake or a bad decision. In the long run, these things are not important. You learn from them. What matters is how you recover. If you are lucky enough to live a long life, as I have been, you learn to pause and look back on what you have accomplished. For me, this accomplishment is not my net worth but the ways that experiences have enriched my life and taught me lessons that in turn have enabled me to improve the lives of others. What could be better than that?

Shortly after I learned that Americana Hotels was being sold, I was traveling for company business. While waiting in O'Hare airport, I went through the phone messages that had come in that day. One was from Vic Appleby, the former sales director from Americana in New York whom I had fired. I hadn't spoken to him in years. He was now the sales director for the Tollman-Hundley Hotel company. I had no idea why he was calling.

I called him from a payphone in the airport.

"Tollman-Hundley just purchased fifty Days Inns," Appleby told me.

Investors Henry Silverman and Saul Steinberg of Reliance Capital Group in New York had purchased the Days Inn of America company and were selling franchises to Tollman-Hundley and other companies. Appleby told me that Reliance Capital Group wanted to hire a new president and chief operating officer of Days Inn. Stanley Tollman and Monty Hundley, who were now heavily invested in the Days Inn company, had asked Appleby if he knew anyone who could fill the position.

"I suggested you," Appleby said.

I was impressed that Appleby thought of me after I had terminated him, and I was also glad that I had called him back rather than tossing his message aside.

I told him I was interested in the position.

After an interview in Chicago and a meeting with Henry Silverman and Saul Steinberg in New York, I was offered the job. On April 22, 1985, I became the president and chief operating officer of Days Inn of America and moved to Atlanta. Although I had held a presidency for Americana, that had been short lived. This felt like my first real presidency, in which I had the complete responsibility for operations.

Earning that position was in part the result of a lesson that I had learned: always treat people well. When I terminated Appleby, I needed to have a difficult conversation with him about his performance, but throughout the termination, I had treated him with dignity. He left understanding his shortcomings as an employee but with respect for me personally. It was because of the respect that he had for me that I was considered for the job at Days Inn.

DAYS INN

Days Inn was formed in the 1970s by a devout Baptist, Cecil Day, as a competitor to Holiday Inn in the South. Cecil Day brought a few ideas to Days Inn. First, he focused on offering a lower price (it was originally called Eight Days Inn because it charged just eight dollars per night as opposed to twelve dollars at Holiday Inn). Days Inn was a stripped-down version of Holiday Inn, not offering meeting spaces or a bar. Days Inn also focused on the senior citizen market. It became a successful business, with 250 Days Inns at the time I became the president.

When Cecil Day died, the business passed to his nephew, Richard Kessler, who then sold it to the Reliance Capital Group in September 1984. Henry Silverman became the CEO and had the responsibility of running the Days Inn operations. Silverman made a few changes to the company during the six months that he ran it. He secured liquor licenses so that hotels could add bars—a development that was initially met by protests from the community. He also transformed the business from a management business into a largely franchise business and sold 125 of the franchises to Asian Indian American hotel owners. I had experience with franchises but from the other side of the business—having been a franchisee while working for Americana and Dunfey.

When I became president of Days Inn, Reliance Capital Group's goal was to grow the company. They had never been in the hotel business before, and now they had 250 hotels, most of which were franchised. They wanted to grow to a total of five hundred hotels in five years. Expanding meant building and creating our own product, which was a process that took years.

"Look," I said to Henry Silverman, "new construction takes too long. We can't build two hundred fifty hotels in five years." I offered a different plan. "We can go into the conversion business. We could buy existing hotels and work on penetrating the major markets." I told Silverman that we should grow the brand by purchasing in key cities in the United States and building brand awareness.

Silverman didn't know the hotel business well, but he was willing to take suggestions. He didn't suffer from the syndrome that affects many bosses: needing to be the author of all great ideas. If an employee presented a good plan, Silverman was willing to put it into action, and he was financially brilliant. We worked well together: he made the big financial decisions and left the operations and marketing to me.

He liked my idea about penetrating the major markets. He bought properties in New York City, Chicago, Minneapolis, Detroit, and Boston and turned the southern Days Inn company into a national chain almost overnight.

THE 800 NUMBER

I spent my first months at Days Inn learning about the operations of the company. I began to uncover inefficiencies, and one of those was in the 800 number.

When I started at Days Inn, the company primarily used an 800 number as their distribution system. The number produced about 40 percent of their business. Many hotel companies—including Americana and Sonesta—had 800 numbers that were run by call centers that booked rooms. The call center for Days Inn was located in Atlanta and had a terrible employee turnover of above 40 percent. We needed to hire people better suited to the positions.

My solution was to hire senior citizens, who were more likely to stay in the jobs long term. People in the industry didn't hire seniors because they believed that elderly employees would become ill, would be unable to adapt to new technologies, or were generally lazy. We proved all those stereotypes wrong. Within a year, 75 percent of our 125-person staff was over fifty-five, and some were in their eighties. We also hired people with disabilities and women from a women's shelter. Human resources provided computer training for the new employees and offered support. Our turnover rate dropped dramatically, to less than 10 percent.

The strategy won the company a Points of Light award from President George H. Bush, and the *New York Times* featured our hiring practices in an article. It was not only good for company morale but also benefited the larger community. When you're doing the right thing from within a company, employees love being there—they love that their work has greater purpose and that it connects them to a community they respect. When they are happy, they stay and do good work for the company.

As we grew, we eventually opened an additional call center in Knoxville, Tennessee, that was staffed by both seniors and students from the University of Tennessee. Our brand, and the number of hotels we owned, were both growing exponentially.

ASIAN AMERICAN HOTEL ASSOCIATION

There were two major areas on which I needed to focus my efforts to improve the overall operations and reputation of Days Inn. One was sales. Expanding the sales force would help to build the hotel brand so that we could penetrate larger markets. I grew the sales department from five to thirty employees who were based all over the country. John Snodgrass led the sales team, which included very successful future executives in the business: Greg Casserly, Steve Romanello, brothers Tim and Michael Muir, and many other people well known even in today's business. Soon we were selling 300 to 400 franchises a year, one year selling 550. By 1990, we had 1,500 Days Inns.

The other area that I focused on was creating a service organization to support the franchisees. The company needed to have good relations with the franchisees so that the franchisees themselves became salespeople for the company. My leadership tactics—based on what Dr. Jervis taught me at Dunfey—were identifying inefficiencies, setting specific and achievable goals, and implementing strategies to make the company more efficient. I improved the franchise approval process, making it efficient and accessible so that while other companies were selling thirty to forty franchises a year, we were selling hundreds. I also formed a franchise service department, something no other company had, to service the franchisee community and thereby nearly eliminating franchisee/franchisor relationship problems.

"You've got a lot of curry palaces," Dan Danielli, a guru of the economy lodging business, told me.

This language caught me off guard.

Most of our franchisees were the first-generation Americans who had come to the United States in the 1960s and 1970s. They often ran the hotels as a family business and lived in the back.

I had little experience with the Asian Indian American population. During the next two years, I got to know several of the franchisees. They were facing terrible discrimination on multiple levels. Many couldn't get mortgages or franchises from other companies. People in the hotel business claimed that franchises owned by Asian Indian owners were dirty, that these franchisees weren't paying their bills, and that they were terrible to work with. I conducted research and found none of these claims to be true.

I met with one of the Indian owners, H. P. Rama from Greenville, South Carolina, who was a leader in the community. He told me about blatant discrimination: roadside signs and billboards announcing "American-owned" that warned guests away from establishments run by Asian Indian Americans, a general lack of acceptance from the hotel industry, and obstacles aimed at his community that were put in place by banks, other hotel companies, and the government. The people in his community weren't being treated like Americans.

We should do something about this, I thought, but I really didn't know what to do. I came to the conclusion that no one had time to properly assist the Asian Indian franchisees.

Then, in 1987, I got a call from a consultant named Lee Dushoff. He told me that he needed a project. "I want to start a national association with Asian Indian franchisees," I told Dushoff.

My idea was that this new organization would model the American Hotel and Lodging Association (AHLA), which was purposed on building community and giving professional recognition to people in the hospitality industry.

Days Inn invested $100,000 to give Dushoff and the Days Inn team time to organize the Asian American Hotel Owners Association, whose purpose it would be to give Asian Americans their rightful place in the hospitality industry. Rama and I played major roles in establishing the organization. We put together my contacts in the industry and members of the Asian Indian community from AHLA, including Ken Hine, the executive director of AHLA; John Crow, an industry consultant; Jerry Merkel, a major hotel trade magazine owner and publisher; and many others. Together, Rama, another franchisee named Ravi Patel, and I traveled around the country, educating franchisees about the organization and selling memberships for an annual fee of twenty-five dollars.

In 1989, we had enough members to hold our first convention, hosting 150 owners from all over the country. We had twelve people on the board, largely comprised of my contacts in the industry, including the head of the American Hotel and Lodging Association, the head trainer of AHLA, and one of the best-known editors of a hotel trade magazine.

In 2019, the annual convention hosted nine thousand members and boasted exhibits from all the major suppliers in the industry. As of 2020, it had nineteen thousand members. The organization transformed the lives of thousands of people and changed the industry's perception of Asian Indian Americans. The Asian Indian American community came to call me Bapu, a name of respect also used for Ghandi.

In 2019, I attended the annual convention, which I sometimes still do. The current president is the first woman to hold the title, Pritti Patel. She gave a speech and introduced a new scholarship for tuition aid to students attending the Leven School of Management, Entrepreneurship, and Hospitality at Kennesaw State University.

I was accused by my competitors of creating the Asian American Hotel Association for monetary and business reasons only, but nothing could be further from the truth. I acted on my principles. I still consider the formation of the Asian American Hotel Association to be the most important accomplishment of my career. It truly solved a problem, improved the industry, and benefited the people in the business.

As president and chief operating officer of Days Inn, I relied on the skills and experiences that I had gained in previous positions, and I learned from the new situations that I encountered. The job truly reflected my personal values and my competency. I knew the importance of the sales department, I valued the people who worked with me and integrated them into the mission of the organization, and I felt confident that my actions and decisions would be supported by my boss, Henry Silverman.

I came to Days Inn with a franchisee perspective, and I learned the franchisor business. I also learned about public markets. Shortly after I started at Days Inn, we took the company public, introducing new possibilities and concerns as well as new strategies that I needed to learn. Once the company was in the public market, I had to work with market analysts, and to do that, I needed to know the financial aspects of the company inside and out. I studied. I learned about the delicate line between discretion and protecting the company as well as the legal and moral obligations to the shareholders—who were now invested in the company. I also applied my knowledge of sales: we were now not only selling to customers and franchisees but also selling shares to the public.

> The great leaders—from professional coaches to CEOs—never stop learning.

I was also excited about learning new things and willing to accept unfamiliar challenges. I already knew that I wanted to be the kind of worker who sought experience. There's always something to learn. The great leaders—from professional coaches to CEOs—never stop learning. They learn from observing and listening to their peers, analyzing their own actions and strategies, and listening to clients and employees. They are also always looking for new strategies to apply. They are not satisfied with the status quo because they know that the status quo is a prescription for failure. I came to Days Inn with that understanding, and it paid off with major success. In the years that I was president, Days Inn went from a little southeastern company with some hotels in California to a major international player with licenses in China, India, Mexico, and Canada. I was proud of the success of the company as well as the many positive ways that I was able to impact a larger community while I was there.

TOLLMAN-HUNDLEY

In December 1989, Silverman sold Days Inn to Tollman-Hundley, who owned fifty franchises. Silverman called to tell me that he had sold the company and to offer to negotiate my new contract.

"You don't have to do that for me," I told Silverman. "I love the job and I'm going to stay anyway."

It was a big mistake. I didn't know Stanley Tollman or Monty Hundley well and had no idea what kind of leaders they would be.

Within the first six months of owning the company, Tollman and Hundley stopped paying their royalties, bills, and mortgage debt on the fifty hotels that they owned. Meanwhile, they were draining Days Inn to fund other entities that they owned. We began to receive late payment notices and fees. AT&T, who owned our 800 number, was not being paid on time.

I met with Tollman and Hundley and told them that they needed to pay their bills. They agreed but still made no payments.

A few months later, the situation had escalated. I went to see a lawyer friend in Boston and told him about the problem. "What they're doing is illegal," he told me. At the time, the company was private but held public bonds and was obligated to certain rules. He told me to try again to get Tollman and Hundley to repay the money they had taken. When that again did not work, the lawyer said, "You better get out of there before you find yourself involved in a federal lawsuit."

It was good advice. I resigned from the job I loved. Had I let Silverman negotiate my contract, I would have walked away with something. Instead, I left with nothing.

Eventually Days Inn went bankrupt. Years later, Stanley Tollman and Monty Hundley were prosecuted on unrelated charges of similar conduct in other business dealings and convicted of fraud, conspiracy to commit bank fraud, lying to banks, and tax evasion. Monty Hundley was sentenced to jail time, and Stanley Tollman fled the country.

My parting with Days Inn had a terrible psychological impact on me. My presidency there had been my favorite job, and I was forced to flee as I watched the company that I built fall apart. A friend suggested that I see a psychologist. When I arrived at the therapist's office, he took one look at me and said, "Who died?" The Days Inn had been like my child. Recovering from the loss took months and was not easy.

Although I had lost a lot—both financially and emotionally—I had been fortunate to be in a position to leave when the company acted against my principles. Three weeks after I left Days Inn, the hotel's lawyer, Joel Buckberg, called me and said that he would like to see me; we hadn't had a chance to say goodbye. We met for lunch. Joel was still working for Days Inn. "How can you stay and work with these people?" I asked.

"I have a sick child," he told me. "I need to take care of the people I love. I need this job."

Sometimes people are not free to make principled choices. You have to tolerate and understand that truth. Part of embracing personal freedom is accepting that everybody will not live their lives according to the way you live yours. People are dealing with personal situations and concerns. The right thing for me was not the right thing for Joel. I understood.

HENRY SILVERMAN

I called Henry Silverman before I left Days Inn for advice. Silverman was working for Blackstone at the time. He was about to buy the Howard Johnson's and Ramada brands, and he asked if I would like to work with him again. He offered me 10 percent of the company, a raise, a bonus, and a major stock option if the company went public. The company would be located in Atlanta.

I accepted the job. Things were looking up.

A couple of days later, I came home from a celebratory dinner with Andrea to a phone call from Silverman. "I have bad news. I can't give you the job," Silverman told me.

Tollman-Hundley had accused Silverman of poaching me from Days Inn and threatened Blackstone with a lawsuit. I hadn't signed a noncompete agreement, but Blackstone didn't want trouble.

Instead, Silverman offered to pay me $25,000 per month to work as a consultant. I would help to organize the overhead structure for his company, Hospitality Franchise Systems. He supported me financially for the next four months until I found another job.

When Days Inn finally went bankrupt, long after I left, Silverman bought it back. Along with Ramada and Howard Johnson's, it became a part of his company.

IN THE END

I learned a great deal from my experience with Days Inn—both from building the company and from its eventual failure. The success of a company is dependent on the leadership. Good leadership must be maintained. An organization can be led well to the result of tremendous success, and the leadership can change and completely undo all the advances.

I lead and manage people from my value structure. I let them work, let them be creative and think differently, and give them opportunities. As a leader, I view my job as one to get employees ready for their next jobs, not to stand in the way of their next jobs. My job is to help the people with whom I work be successful. I don't hover or micromanage—practices that make employees wary and slow creative processes. I let my employees do things in their own ways. In most cases, when they are successful, the company is also successful. It's a long game that pays off in dependable relationships, loyalty, and trust. Business is more like novels than balance sheets: they depend on people and characters more than numbers.

Part of being a good leader is making a good choice in hiring people. As I continued in the business and worked with more people, I was able to make decisions about whom I worked well with or which employees would be best suited to specific positions. I hired people with whom I had worked in the past and knew I could count on. I didn't hire people because I like them; I hired people who could get the results. I hired disruptive people— you want disruption, innovation, and breaks in the status quo—but not destructive people.

> Leadership is not a game of math or even logic; it is human and based on emotions and values.

As a leader, it is also important to accept that you can't be right all the time. You must learn to acknowledge your own failures. It's good to have a sense that you're not perfect. Leadership is not a game of math or even logic; it is human and based on emotions and values. As humans, we are responding to things in the moment to the best of our abilities.

It is difficult to teach leadership, although many MBA programs attempt to do so. Good leadership cannot be boiled down to a particular set of rules. Instead, it is like parenting. No one really teaches you to be a parent. You learn from watching others—including your own parents—and learn from experiences as they arise. You come to know and reveal your principles as you go and to develop values and goals to support those. I believe in personal freedom. I believe in valuing people. I lead the way that I wish to be led.

Lessons Learned

54. If you have to terminate an employee, never take their dignity away.

55. The status quo is a prescription for failure.

56. Strong sales departments can make all the difference in the success of a company.

57. Expand the visibility of your brand using major markets.

58. In a bad situation, you must know that others cannot and will not take the actions that you will take yourself.

59. Hire disruptive people, not destructive people.

60. Remember to treat everyone the way you would like to be treated if you were in the same situation.

CHAPTER 10

TOO OLD? 1989–2005

AN OFFER FROM HOLIDAY INN

In 1989, Holiday Inn Worldwide was sold by the Promus Hotel Corporation in Memphis, Tennessee, to a British company called Bass PLC, a brewer that primarily owned pubs but that had franchised a few Holiday Inns in Europe and was interested in further exploring the hospitality business. Bryan Langton, who was based in London, was the Bass PLC head of operations for the Holiday Inn Group in Europe. After Bass PLC purchased Holiday Inn Worldwide, Langton decided to move the Holiday Inn operations from Memphis to Atlanta, and I got a call from a search firm. Holiday Inn was looking for a president for their franchising division to direct their franchising globally.

I had experience in the franchising business from Days Inn as well as experience working internationally. Bryan Langton arranged to interview me.

Langton was an impressive businessman. He understood the hospitality business from operational and developmental standpoints.

He offered to pay me what I was making at Days Inn. The office was in Atlanta—fifteen minutes from where I was living. I took the job.

Holiday Inn Worldwide was a much larger company than Days Inn, with about twenty-five hundred properties to Days Inn's fifteen hundred—many managed, most franchised. It was a traditional, large company—the largest I'd worked for other than American Airlines. They had a big headquarters with enormous overhead. I reported directly to Langton, and I had people reporting to me from the franchise department on a global scale.

EXPRESS

The Holiday Inn Worldwide company was not in trouble when I was hired. Often if the company is not in trouble, the leaders and investors in the company don't worry about it. They are reactive rather than proactive. But I scrutinized the company to look for possible improvements, although the company was doing well.

When I went to work for Holiday Inn, they were coming out with a new product called Holiday Inn Express. In the hospitality business, there are full-service properties with restaurants, bars, and meeting and conference spaces, and there are select-service properties that often have a breakfast room but little else other than guest rooms. The Holiday Inn Express line represented select-service properties. The initial trial of Holiday Inn Express was three older Holiday Inns that had been converted into Express establishments.

The new hotel line was created in response to a general lack of growth. Holiday Inn was doing fine, but it was not doing better each year. They had been selling only twenty-five to thirty new franchises annually. Holiday Inn devised standards for the new line of Express hotels and was franchising both to franchisees who invested in new construction and to those who converted older properties. The company hoped that Holiday Inn Express would revitalize the company and bring additional business, but it also caused stress for existing franchisees who saw the brand extension as potential competition.

I was asked to analyze the Holiday Inn Express concept. The Holiday Inn Express standard was a minimum of 120 rooms, each of which included a hot breakfast. I knew that the brand couldn't be profitable with that structure. Competitors allowed smaller establishments of down to eighty rooms and only asked franchisees to provide a cold grab-and-go breakfast. The Holiday Inn Express model would eliminate smaller franchisees and alienate some who could not contend with providing a hot breakfast. I told Langton, and he agreed. We needed to change the model.

My next concern was the sales force: we didn't have enough salespeople to proliferate a new market and sell the Holiday Inn Express brand. Langton agreed again.

I hired salespeople who had worked for me at Days Inn as well as management people who could lead the sales effort, including Steve Romanello and Tim and Michael Muir. We built a strong sales organization of twenty-five to thirty people. The Holiday Inn previously had five.

The Holiday Inn was also currently charging only 4 percent in royalties to franchisees. Most other franchisors charged 5 percent. I was shocked that no one else at Holiday Inn had known that 5 percent was the industry standard. I knew that the product was worth the increased royalties and that this change would bring an overall profit increase of up to 20 percent for the company.

We could increase the royalty percentages as contracts renewed. Again, Langton agreed with me, but he charged me with announcing the increase to the Franchise Advisory Committee that represented the franchisees.

I met with the Franchise Advisory Committee and the franchisees. I announced the raise in royalty fees from 4 percent to 5 percent upon the renewal of their contracts as well as the 5 percent standard royalty fee for new Holiday Inn Express franchises.

There were expected objections. Some franchise owners said that they would not renew their contracts. However, I had a lot of leverage. A 5 percent royalty fee was competitive with other franchisors, and we now offered effective sales to bring business to franchisees from both our 800 number and our marketing campaign. The franchisees were still getting a good deal, and most stayed.

I then turned my attention to inefficiencies in the company. I attended a franchise approval meeting where the committee of thirty people who met every six weeks in Memphis reviewed applications. This method was flawed for several reasons. First, the meetings were too infrequent—six weeks was a long time to wait to have an application reviewed. Second, flying thirty committee members to Memphis every six weeks was a big expense to the company. Also, a thirty-person committee was too large. It meant that there were thirty people looking for reasons to reject an application—the meeting that I observed was absurd. With the process that was in place, only thirty new franchises were being approved annually. I changed the process dramatically, forming a five-person committee based in Atlanta who could meet to review applications as they were submitted.

I next began to look for inefficiencies in the structure of the company. I found a fifteen-person credit department whose purpose, I learned, was to check the credit of franchise applicants. When somebody builds or purchases a hotel, they secure a mortgage from a bank, and the bank completes a thorough credit check. Having Holiday Inn check applicants' credit was redundant and delayed the franchise approval process. I eliminated the department.

With all these changes in place, Holiday Inn went from selling thirty franchises a year to selling three hundred. Langton was pleased and so was I. I also developed a franchise service department similar to the one at Days Inn and got to know many of the franchisees, who I admired for their entrepreneurial spirit and successes.

LOSING CUSTOMERS

I worked closely with an executive at Holiday Inn named Kirk Kinsell. One day he came into my office and said, "I don't know why we lose customers."

I knew why. I created a hand-drawn chart (see appendix) for him that pontificated a theory of why businesses generally lose customers.

The idea was this: When businesses start, they are externally focused, or they are focused on the needs of the customers. As they develop, they become more internally focused, which means that leaders and departments are satisfying their own needs and desires and those of the organization rather than working to satisfy the needs and desires of the customers. Leaders are no longer thinking about the end result—the interaction with the customer—and instead focus on the internal process. This problem grows with the company: the bigger the company, the worse the problem. Management becomes oriented toward internal workings rather than external outcomes. The customer is forgotten.

Holiday Inn had built a large bureaucracy that was standing in the way of customer satisfaction. They were also an older, well-established company that had become set in a specific way of doing things. They rarely took the time to consider why they did things as they did, or if the way that they were doing things was still working. I needed to refocus Holiday Inn onto external needs and goals.

In franchise companies, the customer is not always the end user—the person who eats in the restaurant or stays in the hotel room—rather, the customer is often the franchisee. When the franchisee is content and satisfied, they will usually take care of the customer. Companies must pay attention both to the end users and to those people who deliver services to the end users.

COMPLAINTS

I received a letter of complaint from a customer who had a terrible stay at the Holiday Inn in Acapulco. The customer had sent several letters and received no reply. I followed up on the complaint and found another inefficiency at Holiday Inn.

Holiday Inn had a department of fifteen people dealing with complaints from all the hotels. There were a lot of hotels and a lot of complaints. When I asked about the specific complaint that I had received, I was told that the complaint department had informed the franchisee and that the franchisee was responsible for contacting the customer.

"How often do you contact the appropriate franchisee when you receive a complaint?" I asked.

"Always," I was told.

"How often do you get second or third letters from the same customers about the same complaints?"

"All the time," I was told.

The franchisees mainly ignored the complaints in the hope that the customers would forget their grievances. Sometimes, after receiving multiple letters, they would act.

"That's not the way to handle complaints," I said.

I decided to change the system, enacting lessons that I had learned when I worked for Dunfey. "If a customer is not satisfied with their stay, we refund their money and bill the franchisee," I told the complaint department.

If the franchisee had a reasonable dispute with the complaint, the company would cover the bill. If not, the franchisee would be responsible for the refund. If the franchisees did not comply, Holiday Inn would remove them from the reservation system.

This simplified process for dealing with complaints also meant that we could downsize the complaint department from fifteen to five employees. Refunding costs to customers that were not refunded by the franchisees cost the company about $100,000 per year; decreasing the size of the complaint department saved us about $400,000 per year. The changes that we were making were profitable.

TOO OLD?

At the end of my second year with Holiday Inn, Langton promoted me to president of the Americas, a position responsible for all the Holiday Inns in North, South, and Central America, including the Caribbean. While many of the Holiday Inns were franchises, the company also managed 250 hotels. Because I had previous experience in management, as well as the franchise business, I was well suited for the position.

A year and a half later, I was promoted to president and chief operating officer for Holiday Inn Worldwide—the number two guy—responsible for all the regional offices and hotels around the world. I already had experience with international markets from my work at Sonesta and franchising experience from Days Inn; now I also knew the goals and workings of Holiday Inn.

As chief operating officer, I went to the Holiday Inn headquarters in London with Langton every six weeks. I got along well with the people in the corporate office. My next promotion should have been to head of operations when Bryan Langton retired. I was completely confident that I was capable of doing that job well.

At the beginning of 1995, Langton told me that he was planning to retire at the end of the year. "I'm going to be sixty," he said.

Months went by, and Langton did not discuss his retirement or replacement with me. Finally, in the summer, I asked, "What's going to happen when you leave?"

I expected him to say, "I hope you'll take the job." Instead, he said nothing.

Then I asked, "Can you explain why you're retiring at age sixty? You're still young."

"The company has a regulated retirement age of sixty," he told me.

I couldn't believe it. The regulation had been in place since the company was started in 1714. "In 1714, nobody lived to be sixty," I told Langton. "It's an absurd rule."

"That's the way it is," Langton said.

It was a small example of the main issue at Holiday Inn: they relied on established structures and legacy systems without considering whether they were effective and appropriate in the current situation. This happens in companies all the time. They grow into bureaucracies with structures and regulations that become obstacles to employees rather than support systems that allow people to do their jobs effectively.

In August, I asked Langton point-blank, "When you leave, am I going to get your job?"

"No," he said. "You're fifty-eight years old and you have to retire at sixty. They won't put you in the position for two years."

I had no future at Holiday Inn. It was ironic that after starting the program at Days Inn to employ seniors, I would be denied a promotion at Holiday Inn based on age.

After five years at Holiday Inn, I left. Brian Langton was still there. I went to his office to say goodbye. He hugged me and said, "Mike, I couldn't have done it without you." It was the first positive reinforcement, other than formal promotions, that I received from him in all the years I worked there.

A few years after I left Holiday Inn, I happened to be on a plane with the chief financial officer of Bass PLC. "The biggest mistake we ever made was not giving you Langton's job," he confessed to me. After I left, the company had difficulties finding leaders who understood the hospitality business. "It's cost us millions of dollars," the CFO told me. Holiday Inn has since extended the retirement age.

US FRANCHISE SYSTEMS

I wasn't ready to retire. In September 1995, I got a call from my nephew—Andrea's brother's son—Neal Aronson. Neal worked at Drexel Burnham as an analyst and with the private equity company Odyssey Partners. He understood corporate finance, but he had no operating experience. He was leaving his job with the hope of starting his own business, allowing him to be on the principle side of private equity as opposed to the investor side. He asked if I would be his partner. I agreed. When I retired from Holiday Inn Worldwide, we formed a company called US Franchise Systems.

There was an economy hotel brand called Microtel with twenty-two hotels. The founder had died, and we bought the company with the idea of building a franchise conglomerate. We raised $17 million: $4 million went to buy Microtel, and $13 million went to pay the overhead and build the franchise company. We modeled a combination of strategies that I had learned at Days Inn and Holiday Inn to build Microtel and other small brands.

I became the CEO and chairman, with Neal as the CFO. My sons Jon and Robert joined the business, as did Neal's brother, Steven. It was a family affair. In addition, I brought other people on board with whom I had worked at Days Inn to head the sales force, including Steve Romanello, the Muir brothers, and Debbie Campbell. We wrote a franchisee-oriented franchise agreement that later won awards from the American Franchisee Association.

US Franchise Systems was an entrepreneurial organization that Neal and I were building from the ground up. Now, rather than being charged with turning around a failing business, Neal and I were creating the organization and operation; we weren't correcting other people's mistakes, we were making our own—and we made plenty of them. This was not a bureaucracy. There was no structure of committee after committee needed to make a decision or approve an idea. I structured the business with very low overhead, a large sales force, and an equally sized service force to support the franchisees. During the previous decades, I had learned something about what made businesses work, and now I had the opportunity to apply what I had learned.

At some point Neal said to me, "You could have raised a lot more money based on your reputation and built and run ten or twenty of your own hotels rather than franchising other brands."

But I loved the franchise business more than operations. Also, I had already built and run hotels with Silverman at Days Inn. "I don't want to be in the management business," I told my nephew. I had learned something about the different aspects of the business and knew what was right for me. What I wanted to do was create franchise systems, market and sell the brand, and provide great service and support for the brand. I didn't want to run hotels. We could build our company faster and do the job better by concentrating on franchising.

Once we were established, we could grow by buying additional systems (not necessarily systems in the hotel business).

Neal and I started developing our business. We bought the Hawthorn Suites brand, which competed in the extended-stay market. To be profitable, we would need to grow both the Microtel and the Hawthorn Suites brands. We did well the first year. Because we received an initial fee for each new franchise sold, we were able to reduce our loss for purchases while we were waiting for new hotels to open that would pay royalties. New Hawthorn Suites were mainly converted older buildings, which meant that they opened more quickly than the Microtels that were new construction and took time to build.

After success in our first year, Neal and I decided to take the company public in December 1996. Based in part on my reputation for success in the hospitality industry, we had a good public offering. We raised enough money to repay our investors their original loan that we had taken. The following year, in 1997, we made a secondary offering and raised $40 million—the stock went from $10.50 in the initial offering to $24.00 after the secondary offering, growing our value to $400 million from our original $17 million investment. We were opening hotels and growing the brands. The company was doing well.

A TURN

Two things happened then that changed the trajectory of US Franchise Systems. The first was that Hilton bought Homewood Suites—a brand that competed with our Hawthorn Suites brand. Hilton became aggressive in trying to dominate the market. They convinced one of our Hawthorn Suites franchisees to convert five of his franchises—the best properties in our brand—into Homewood Suites. Because the franchisee had broken his agreement, we collected liquidated damages, but the damage to the Hawthorn Suites brand was not recoverable.

Microtel, however, was still expanding. In only a couple of years, we went from twenty to two hundred franchises. Considering that this was new construction, it was extremely fast growth. Our second stock offering in 1997 raised $40 million. I told Neal that I wanted to start looking at small franchise companies to buy—not only hotels but also restaurants and other industry brands with thirty to fifty establishments. We had infrastructure in place, and we could focus on expansion.

Neal disagreed with my vision for the company's future. People on Wall Street were recommending that we stay in the hotel business. We were approached by the Best Inns of America company, which both owned and franchised hotels. They wanted to sell us the company. The deal they offered was for the purchase of their management company as well as some of their assets and a few of the franchises. I hated the deal and the proposition of going into management, but Neal was in favor. In the end, we bought Best Inns of America for $40 million. It was disastrous for US Franchise Systems. I had made a mistake by not stating my opinions strongly enough to convince Neal.

Best Inns of America was problematic. We couldn't sell the brand to franchisees and had to manage the hotels ourselves. It didn't work, and it didn't fit into the original mission of US Franchise Systems, which was solely to grow brands that could be franchised and managed outside of our company.

By 2000, US Franchise Systems was not doing well. We were still selling Microtel and Hawthorn franchises, and I was working on selling the Best Inns of America company. Our stock was hovering in a range between fifteen and seventeen dollars.

Then the terrorist attacks of September 11, 2001, arrested the nation. Construction stopped.

In October, an analyst reported on the company: we might not grow fast enough to meet expectations. After reading the report, I knew that we would not make our projected earnings by the end of the year; we weren't going to be able to open enough new hotels. "I think we ought to disclose," I said to Neal. I didn't want people buying our stock because they anticipated that we would make our projected profit, a goal that was obviously not attainable.

Neal spoke to an outside lawyer for the company. The lawyer said that we were not obligated to report earnings until February. "Maybe something will happen by February to change the situation," Neal said.

"I'm telling you that I know now that we're not going to make these numbers by the end of the year," I told Neal. "I can tell you which hotels are going to open and what the royalty stream is going to be. I know we won't make the numbers."

"We don't have to report that until February," Neal said. "Maybe we'll make an acquisition before then."

I knew that we couldn't make an acquisition in the next four months. Even if we did, an acquisition wouldn't change our profits much. "We have to disclose," I insisted.

A couple of days later, I received a telephone message from an analyst at Bear Stearns who was researching US Franchise Systems as part of report that would inform his company's investments for clients. He told me that Bear Stearns was going to upgrade our stock the following week. "I just wanted to let you know in advance," the message said.

I took the message to Neal's office. "How do I respond to this knowing we're not going to make our earnings?" I asked.

We spoke with the lawyer again. He instructed me not to talk to the analyst. Anything I told him would be considered insider information. "You're stuck," the lawyer said. "Don't return the call."

I agreed not to return the call, but I said to Neal and the lawyer together, "I want to disclose now that the company is not going to make the projected profits by end of the year."

Neal was concerned. Our company had a good story that reflected its projected performance rather than our actual performance. If shareholders knew that we were not going to meet our projections, they would sell, and the stock's value would be cut in half or worse.

"I don't care," I said. "I don't want a lawsuit. Someone is going to ask me if I knew what was going to happen, and the answer is that I did know."

"OK," Neal agreed. He called the company lawyer again, this time to tell him to report that US Franchise Systems was not going to meet its projected profits. The lawyer wrote the press release and sent it to us for approval.

I was sitting in my office, holding the press release that was going out that night after the market closed, when the analyst called again from Bear Stearns. He left another message telling me that he was upgrading our stock that day. I still could not give him the information that he needed.

The press release went out that evening. The next day we received a $50,000 bill from the lawyer for processing the release, and I got another call from the analyst, which I answered this time. He was irate. He yelled and called me names. "Why didn't you tell me?" he asked.

I said to him, "If I had told you, I would have been guilty of revealing insider information. I didn't answer your phone calls hoping you would think something was wrong. That was the only thing I could do."

He called me another name and hung up.

Years later, I was told by a Wall Street executive that I should have told the analyst about our situation. "I was informed by a lawyer not to say anything," I said. He responded that other CEOs give information like that to analysts all the time. I still feel that I made the right decision. I took the most ethical actions possible in the moment.

TWO CHOICES

After a month of difficult consideration, I called Neal into my office. He is my nephew and a wonderful person. I love him. I said to him, "You have two choices. You can leave the company, or we can sell the company."

Neal and I had had a difference of opinion that, at its core, was about critical values. I had felt that the right thing to do was to immediately report the status of the company so that investors had time to respond regardless of what that meant to our success; Neal had believed that we should follow the letter of the law and wait as a means of preserving our own capital. Our different reactions represented something more than that single decision; it was a divergence in our way of doing business. My entire business career rested on a reputation that I built by acting and behaving according to principles in which I believed. I couldn't be responsible or seen as representing the types of actions that Neal wanted to take, even though those actions were legal.

Neal considered and came back to me. "It will look bad if I leave the company," he said. "I'd rather sell."

We put US Franchise Systems up for sale.

The stock had dropped from eleven dollars to five dollars after the press release came out. Henry Silverman called and offered me seven dollars a share to buy US Franchise Systems, which he would integrate into his own company. "You can come be the president," he offered.

We couldn't get a better offer than that.

On the day we were scheduled to sign the contract, Silverman was notified that he was being sued, and the value of his stock fell. Silverman couldn't go through with his purchase of US Franchise Systems.

Instead, the Hyatt Company, which already owned 11 percent of US Franchise Systems' stock, agreed to purchase the company for five dollars a share.

We had fallen a long way from our peak at twenty-four dollars, but the original investors had still made a lot of money.

Neal began a new company called Roark Capital, which was largely funded by the original investors in US Franchise Systems. It is now a multibillion-dollar company built on the strategy of buying and consolidating franchise companies.

I stayed as the CEO of US Franchise Systems and worked for Hyatt for the next three years, until 2005.

When I left Hyatt, I thought it was the end of my career in hospitality. I had earned enough during my career to help my sons and to save for a comfortable retirement. Things had gone very well, but they could have been a lot better.

Lessons Learned

61. Understand why businesses lose customers (see appendix).

62. If you don't handle complaints immediately, they grow larger in time.

63. The franchisee is your customer. The franchisee's customer is the end user.

64. If you have a great brand, the franchisee will pay the royalty.

65. Be careful not to encroach on a franchisee's territory if you want good relationships.

66. Be fair to all customers, and they will honor you if you do not get positive reinforcement.

67. If you do not get positive reinforcement until the end of your work, give it to others as much as you can while you work.

68. Just because it's legal doesn't mean it's the right thing to do.

CHAPTER 11

RETIREMENT? 2005-2009

RETIREMENT

As I started my retirement, my friend Bernie Marcus, one of the founders of Home Depot, asked if I would run his philanthropic foundation, the Marcus Foundation. I was already a trustee at that time. The Marcus Foundation is a private foundation that makes significant contributions to charitable causes. Bernie wanted me to organize it. He offered me a reasonable salary.

My job was to propose new ways to use the foundation funds in accordance with the pillars of the foundation and to work with the people in grant management. The foundation had a small staff that worked in a family office, which was something to which I was not accustomed. Bernie made decisions about what to fund himself. I was there to administer Bernie's decisions, suggest others, and measure the foundation's accomplishments.

Bernie also asked me to be on the board of the Georgia Aquarium, which was being constructed at the time. I accepted the offer, contributing my knowledge of the hospitality industry to the design of the aquarium—from ideas about creating food and beverage facilities to managing deliveries. Based on my input, Bernie decided to add a large ballroom to the aquarium that could host events and create a revenue stream.

The second year that I was with the Marcus Foundation, I got a call from an old friend from the hotel business by the name of Irwin Chafetz. He was now working for a company called GWV Travel that organized charter travel business. Coincidentally, he was from Boston and had attended my high school, although he was a year my senior.

He was one of the partners, along with the Las Vegas Sands (LVS) Corporation CEO Sheldon Adelson, in COMDEX, the computer expo trade show that was held in Atlanta when I was the president of Days Inn. I didn't know Sheldon well, but I'd had dinner with him and Chafetz in Atlanta a couple of times. Chafetz told me that Sheldon was planning to take LVS public, and he wanted me to join the board. My work at the Marcus Foundation was not taxing—even combined with my duties as a board member for the Georgia Aquarium. I had time to dedicate to the LVS board, but I was apprehensive. I had heard that Sheldon didn't listen to his board members. "If I could be assured that Sheldon is going to consider my ideas, I have the time," I told Chafetz.

I got a call from Sheldon. "I want to assure you that I will listen to my board," Sheldon said. LVS had opened a hotel in Macau and also owned the Venetian in Las Vegas. They were in the process of building the Palazzo in Las Vegas as well as other hotels in Pennsylvania, Singapore, and elsewhere. "I need you on my board," he told me.

The Georgia Aquarium opened in 2005 and had an amazing first year. In the second year, the aquarium began to deteriorate somewhat in terms of its operation. Bernie Marcus asked me to consult on the management of the aquarium. I didn't know much about fish, but I knew a lot about management. I began consulting at the aquarium in 2006. At the end of the year, the CEO left and Bernie asked me to take his place. Now I was CEO of the Georgia Aquarium, and in 2007, I began my service on the board of LVS.

LAS VEGAS SANDS GOES PUBLIC

A year after I joined the board, LVS went public. Because I had run a public company, I knew the process and still had relationships with people at Goldman Sachs—the banker for LVS—and other companies dealing with public markets. LVS was being run by three people: President Bill Weidner, Executive Vice President Brad Stone, and Head of Operations for the Venetian Hotel and Casino in Las Vegas Rob Goldstein. All three were familiar with the gaming business. Bill and Brad also had hotel experience.

The day before the stock went public, we had a final pricing meeting for the stock. Sheldon had forgotten to create a pricing committee.

"I have experience with a pricing committee. I'll be happy to help," I said.

Another board member, Charlie Foreman, also volunteered to be on the committee. Our banker was David Solomon, who is now the CEO of Goldman Sachs. He looked at our proposal for an initial offering of twenty-eight dollars and said, "This offering is too low. I would recommend a price of somewhere between twenty-eight and thirty-one dollars. You are oversubscribed."

Charlie and I agreed that we should take the higher price. If we didn't, people would buy the stock at twenty-eight dollars and sell it at thirty-one dollars or more. It would leave Sheldon and other people selling shares with less money. We took the proposal back to Sheldon.

The highest that Sheldon was willing to sell the stock was at twenty-eight dollars a share. "I don't want people to think that I'm overcharging," Sheldon said.

I explained to Sheldon that he was not overcharging. "What's going to happen is that Goldman Sachs and other companies will buy the stock on the IPO," I told Sheldon. "They're going to make the three-dollar difference instead of you."

Sheldon didn't care. He wanted to sell the stock at a fair price. His values were to not overreach. He cost himself a lot of money. I thought that it was a business mistake, but I respected that he stuck to his principles. Many years later, he told me I was right about that decision. He thought it would benefit people, but it only benefited large institutions. The stock opened at forty-one dollars and in the next few years rose as high as $148.00 a share.

2008

I wasn't in favor of the way the management team—Bill Weidner, Brad Stone, and Rob Goldstein—was running LVS. They would often attend board meetings and, when Sheldon wasn't present, complain about Sheldon's decisions. Sheldon was the genius behind LVS. The management of the company should have supported him. Toward the end of 2007, after listening to Weidner complain about Sheldon in a meeting, I said to Weidner, "The founder's stock that Sheldon gave you is worth seven hundred million. Why don't you just cash out and go and stop complaining?"

"I want to be a billionaire," Weidner answered. That explained his goals and objectives.

Then the company took a turn.

By the summer of 2008, our stock was bouncing around between eight and twelve dollars—the market was anticipating major problems.

At the board meeting in June, Widener arrived with a representative from Goldman Sachs and made an announcement. "I think we're going to run out of cash," he said.

We had a couple of problems. New hotels hadn't opened yet and weren't bringing in revenue, and the profits had decreased at our open hotels. In addition, we were paying interest on our existing loans. Money was going out and not coming in. We were close to breaking loan covenants.

The representative from Goldman Sachs recommended a convertible security. While it would dilute the stock to some degree, it would also give the company a safety net of capital until the new properties opened and boosted the stock price. Sheldon was opposed to anything that would dilute the stock. "Business will get better by September," Sheldon assured everyone. Sheldon owned approximately 70 percent of the stock and had the majority vote, so the board accepted his decision.

In September 2008, Lehman Brothers went bankrupt, the whole market fell apart, and the US economy entered a major recession. LVS was at risk for defaulting on loans. Our stock went down to five dollars per share. Goldman Sachs secured investors and asked Sheldon to contribute $1 billion of his own money. The influx of money and purchases of shares boosted the overall stock value. The move saved the company. It gave us time to both adjust to the recession and pay our bills while we waited for new properties to open and become profitable.

NEW MANAGEMENT?

In September 2008, Sheldon lost confidence in the management team, particularly Weidner. Although it was never proven, people accused Weidner—along with others—of trying to convince investors to remove Sheldon as CEO.

In November, Sheldon asked me to find a replacement for Weidner. He wanted the search kept quiet and therefore didn't want me to use a search firm. "Sheldon," I said, "I'm seventy-one years old. Most of the people I know are either retired or dead." But Sheldon was convinced that I could do it.

I spent the months of November and December searching for a replacement for Weidner. By December, I had found only one interested candidate. He wanted 9 million in stock options—our stock was down to $1.56 per share at that time—and a salary of one dollar per year. Sheldon interviewed the candidate but did not hire him; Sheldon didn't want to give anyone such a large amount of stock options.

In December, I went to Israel for the bar mitzvah of a friend's grandson. Sheldon happened to be in Israel at the same time. Although I was on the board with Sheldon, I didn't know him on a personal level. In Israel, Andrea and I spent time with Sheldon and his wife, Miriam. Sheldon got to know me better, and I came to understand more of Sheldon's values.

By January 2009, LVS was in real turmoil. I regretted that I had not been able to find a candidate for president of LVS who was suitable to Sheldon. Weidner was still there. Our stock was down to $1.40 per share. After a board meeting, Sheldon invited me to his office. There I found his wife and stepdaughter sitting on the couch beside him. "I want you to be the president of the company," Sheldon said to me.

"Sheldon, I'm seventy-one years old," I repeated. "I'm retired. I can't do this job. It's ridiculous."

Sheldon was persistent. "I'll pay you $1 million a year, plus a bonus, and I'll give you three million stock options."

I already had a lot going on—I was now the CEO of the Georgia Aquarium in addition to being on Sheldon's board. Besides, if I took the job as president of LVS, I would need to relocate to Las Vegas—where I had been flying for board meetings. "It won't work," I said.

"Come for two years," Sheldon pleaded. "Help me turn the company around and then you can retire again. I'll give you a private plane, and you can commute from Atlanta."

Sheldon's wife, Miriam, said, "Please. Do us a favor and think about it over the weekend. You'll have a lot of fun here."

It didn't sound like fun. The stock was plummeting and the management was a mess. But as a favor to Sheldon and his family, I spoke to Andrea about the offer.

Andrea almost fainted. "We've been in Atlanta since 1985, the longest we've been anywhere," she said. "Our friends are here. Our kids and grandkids are here."

That was exactly how I felt.

That night, I couldn't sleep. For a long time, I stared through the darkness at the ceiling. Then I glanced at Andrea. She was staring at the ceiling too. "I think you should take this job," she said.

"Why?" I asked.

"You're bored," she said.

"I'm not going to commute for two years," I told her.

"I'll come with you," she said. "We'll move to Las Vegas."

"Really?"

"Yes. I think that it will be an experience."

I needed to talk to Bernie Marcus for advice. The next day I flew to Florida. It was a Sunday morning, and I met Bernie at his house in Saint Andrews.

"I have a job offer," I told him and explained Sheldon's offer.

"You should take it," Bernie said.

I was surprised by his response. It would mean more work for Bernie—he would need to replace me at the aquarium. "Why should I take it?" I asked.

"You'll make a lot of money for Sheldon Adelson, and you'll make money for yourself that will go to help the United States of America and the State of Israel."

Before I left, Bernie said, "Two things. First, I'm going to negotiate your contract with the Las Vegas Sands Corporation. I've known you for thirty years or more, and you've never made a decent deal for yourself. You're no good at it. We're going to sit here and make a list of what you want, and when the corporation doesn't agree, you're going to come back to me and I'm going to tell you what to do. Second, I want you to move here to Saint Andrews when you finally retire so that I can see you more often."

I agreed to both terms. Together we made a list of my job requirements. My biggest concern was that I wouldn't be able to make LVS successful and that I would spend two years working hard and my options in the company would be worth nothing.

"What is your net worth now?" Bernie asked.

It was $8 to $10 million.

"What you want is for the company to guarantee that in two years you will make at least $10 million so that you'll double your net worth."

"Bernie, it's never going to happen," I said.

"Trust me," Bernie said. "Call Sheldon's man and tell him what you want."

Charlie Foreman was officially negotiating my contract with LVS. Sitting with Bernie at his house in Florida, I called Charlie and read him the list of requirements on which Bernie and I had decided.

"I'll have to talk to Sheldon," Charlie said.

Charlie called back twenty minutes later. Sheldon had agreed to my terms, but the company could not guarantee that I would walk away with $10 million if my options were worth less. Such a guarantee would need to be disclosed publicly, and Sheldon was worried that it would show lack of confidence in the company. "He'll back the guarantee with his personal funds," Charlie said. "He can't give you anything in writing. He'll give you his handshake."

"Take his handshake. Take the job," Bernie said.

I became president of Las Vegas Sands Corporation March 9, 2009. It was a decision that I would not have made had not my wife and Bernie Marcus convinced me that it was a good idea. They were both looking out for my best interests: my wife was concerned about my happiness, and Bernie was thinking of the United States of America and the State of Israel.

Lessons Learned

69. You can take a handshake if you trust the person.

70. Do not be afraid of what looks impossible.

71. You need to have close advisers who have your best interests at heart and no other agenda.

72. Age makes no difference if you are up to the challenge.

73. Never underestimate your experience to get things done.

74. Relationships that are built in the past will always come back to help, not haunt, you.

167

CHAPTER 12

LAS VEGAS SANDS, 2009–2014

PRESIDENT OF LAS VEGAS SANDS CORPORATION

During the weeks before I started my presidency with LVS, I began to build a team of people who could work with me. I called former employees and colleagues. In particular, I reconnected with Gunther Hatt with whom I had worked at Dunfey, Americana, and Sonesta. He knew the Asian markets and had retired in Thailand. "Do you want to go to work?" I asked.

"Sure," Hatt said.

He would become a part of the operating team in Macau.

Then I called Miguel Coder, a terrific operator with a food and beverage background with whom I had worked at Americana and Holiday Inn. "Do you want to go to work?" I asked.

"Sure," Coder said.

Then I called Steve Jacobs with whom I had worked at Holiday Inn. Jacobs was a very intelligent IT designer and consultant who could build reservation and other related systems. I asked if he would consult for LVS.

"Sure," he said.

I started as president of LVS Corporation on March 9, 2009. When I got to Las Vegas, Benny Zin, a retired Israeli brigadier general and friend of Sheldon's, whom Sheldon had hired, joined the team, along with Ken Kay, the new CFO of LVS who was hired in December 2008. Brad Stone and Rob Goldstein were also still there; Goldstein was still managing the Venetian and Palazzo Hotels in Las Vegas, and Stone was responsible for the operations of other properties. The stock was at $1.55 a share. Bill Weidner had been terminated.

When I became president, I took over the general operations for all the properties (a job that had previously belonged to Stone), and Stone left soon thereafter. Both he and Weidner had made a substantial amount of money on their founders' stock.

When I started, the company wasn't making money. Construction had been stopped on four properties, including the Cotai Strip hotels (a four-thousand room Sheridan, a four-hundred-room Saint Regis, and two Shangri-La hotels: one called the Traders with twelve hundred rooms and one called the Shangri-La with six hundred rooms) as well as the property in Bethlehem, Pennsylvania. In addition, the company had started construction on a $5.5 billion hotel and casino in Singapore that we might not have the capital to finish. I had my work cut out for me.

The first week I was on the job, I was called to Wall Street to be introduced in a Goldman Sachs meeting in New York. I knew some of the people in the meeting from my days working for public companies years earlier. The Goldman Sachs employees fired questions at me. "What do you know about the gaming business?" they asked.

I had managed casinos in Aruba and Puerto Rico long ago, and I had been on the board of LVS for years, but I was not an expert in the gaming industry. "I'm not a gaming guy," I told them. "I know hotel operations, and I understand companies. I'm going to do my best to learn about the gaming industry, and I'm also going to rely on those with experience." People like Goldstein, who knew the business well, would be valuable resources.

The representatives from Goldman Sachs were skeptical about my ability to do the job. I needed to prove them wrong.

TRIMMING THE FAT

My first task was to create an analytical team and complete in-depth analyses of the various operations owned by LVS. The first analysis we did was of the Venetian and Palazzo Hotels in Las Vegas as well as the corporate overhead. We found redundancy in job positions as well as generally unnecessary holdings—for example, three warehouses for furniture storage that could be consolidated into one. Rob Goldstein was the general manager of the Venetian and Palazzo. He had a background in gaming but not in hotels. Consequently, there were inefficiencies in the way the hotels were operating. There were many little excesses that added up to a lot of money.

I also hired two new people in the marketing and sales department: Manuel Olaiz, who was the former vice president of sales for a Mexican company of which I was on the board, and Jerry DePitro, who was my director of sales at the Dunfey Company and who had become a tour expert. Together they implemented new strategies in the marketing department to help improve the image of and create sales for the Venetian and Palazzo Hotels.

Then we moved on to Sands China Inc., which included the Sands Hotel and Casino in Macao and the Venetian Hotel in Macao—both of which were open. The analytical team from Las Vegas went to Macao to conduct the same analysis. There we found one of the biggest messes I had ever seen. There were eleven hundred people in the accounting department, three hundred people in the purchasing department, and fifteen people in the government relations department. The excess was staggering. As I sat in my suite in Macao listening to the analytical team's report, I put my head in my hands and said, "I've never seen anything like this."

I knew that Sands China needed new management from the top. I couldn't stay. I needed to return to Las Vegas. Jacobs volunteered to stay and be the CEO of Sands Macao. I also left Hatt, Coder, Ken Kay, and Benny Zin to restructure the operations. It was a success. Between the Sands Macao and the Sands establishments in Las Vegas, we were able to save the corporation $650 million of annual operating expenses in only 120 days after the analytical team was created.

Although Sands China was doing well, Jacobs was not the right person to manage the operations there. He was a brilliant tactician and technically very competent, but he was not a good leader or communicator. He didn't consult with other people at Sands China or with the corporation before making decisions. It made Sands China difficult to manage from afar in the long run, but in the immediate term, the team who worked there vastly improved the operations.

Sheldon saw and appreciated what we had been able to accomplish. One day he came into my office and said, "I don't understand something. When I give people an order, why is it that they don't do it? When you give people an order, they always do it."

I said, "Sheldon, the difference is before I give people an order, I explain the situation and the reasons for taking the action. You make the assumption that people understand the situation and give the order without explanation."

My management style was always to ensure that my employees understood why I was asking them to do something. Taking the time to help people see the reasons and goals for their tasks gained their commitment to getting it done. That strategy had made our transformation of Sands China a success.

I then moved on to the Marina Bay Sands facility in Singapore, which was still under construction. The people who had been hired to manage the operations had the wrong kind of experience. I was concerned. I conferred with Sheldon and he agreed. I needed to find the right people for the jobs.

In the position of president of the hotel, I hired Tom Arasi, a former investment banker with Solomon Brothers, who had also worked in development for Intercontinental Hotels. In the position of executive vice president, I hired Ronan Nissenbaum, who had worked in the hospitality business his entire professional life. Now the Marina Bay Sands was on the right track.

TAKING SANDS CHINA PUBLIC

When I returned from Singapore, I met with analysts from Wall Street to discuss various aspects of LVS operations. An analyst for Merrill Lynch named Sean Kelly offered a strategy for making LVS a success. It included reducing the costs of operations and taking Sands China public on the Hong Kong Stock Exchange. He thought that if the company gained credibility, the stock would go up and the earnings would allow Sands China to finance the facilities that were still under construction.

It sounded like a great idea. Sheldon approved the plan, and we put it into action. At the end of 2010, we took Sands China public and sold 29 percent of the company. We had a pricing meeting in Hong Kong with Jacobs, Kay, Sheldon, representatives from Goldman

Sachs, and others. The representatives from Goldman Sachs recommended that we price the stock at twelve times the EBITDA (earnings before interest, taxes, depreciation, and amortization). Sheldon said he wanted seventeen times the EBITDA. It was three o'clock in the afternoon, and we had to go to the printer at five o'clock. The Goldman Sachs representatives and Sheldon were in a standoff. No one wanted to confront either.

We sat for an hour and nothing happened. I was seated next to Kay and asked him, "How much money do we need to make from the offering to be able to finance the remaining construction on the facilities in Macau, Bethlehem, and Singapore?"

He got out his calculator. "Three point two billion dollars," he said.

"How much would we need to ask for the stock to accrue three point two billion?" I continued.

Kay typed on his calculator again. "Thirteen to fourteen times the EBITDA," he said.

I looked at the representatives from Goldman Sachs and then at Sheldon. Neither objected.

"That's where we'll price the stock," I said.

Then we had to sell the stock, which required Sheldon, Jacobs, and me to meet with potential buyers around the world and promote the facilities in Macao. While we were traveling, Jacobs's relationship with Sheldon deteriorated dramatically. Jacobs wanted to be in charge, and he frequently took control of the meetings without giving deference to Sheldon or consulting with me. While the trip was detrimental to Jacobs's and Sheldon's relationship, it fared well for Sands China. The reception from potential buyers was positive. By the time we arrived in San Francisco for the concluding meeting and final pricing, things were looking good.

We arrived at the final pricing meeting at the Saint Regis Hotel to find the representatives from Goldman Sachs looking miserable. The Asian markets had plummeted. I knew that it might mean that they wouldn't offer us a good price for the Macao Sands stock.

"What's your offer?" I asked the Goldman Sachs representatives.

"The best we can do is thirteen times the EBITDA."

Thirteen times the EBITDA was the minimum that we needed. We raised $3.2 billion. The company cleared the hurdle. We sold 29 percent of the Sands Macao stock and had the cash flow and the ability to finance and complete the construction of all the hotels in the portfolio. The company was doing well, and the stock immediately went up to fifteen dollars.

SINGAPORE

I then focused on Marina Bay Sands in Singapore. I spent a great deal of time there with the two people I had hired to run the facilities: Nissenbaum and Arasi. Eventually I also brought in a new director of sales and marketing, Mike Lee, with whom I had worked at the Americana Hotels in the 1980s.

Many of the problems with the Marina Bay Sands had to do with the physical construction and design of the facility. Once I identified this, I began to work with the architect, Moshe Safdie, who was world renown, to reimagine the space. It eventually became one of the most successful products of its kind in the world, with a museum, casino, banquet halls, and big retail shopping center.

The agreement with Singapore included a free outdoor light and water show that would enhance the aesthetics of the facility's exterior and attract passersby. It was a $15 million endeavor with a company in Australia that, once complete, won numerous awards. It was a great success. Before opening Marina Bay Sands, the Sands Corporation earned $700 million of EBITDA during the soft opening. In the years since, the corporation has consistently earned between $1.4 and $1.5 billion of EBITDA.

Things were going well. Sheldon extended my two-year contract for two more years, then extended it two more years again to end in December 2014. The last year that I was with the company, LVS earned $5.4 billion of EBITDA, and it was $700 million at the end of 2008.

Because Sheldon Adelson has a reputation of being difficult to work with, I am often asked about my working relationship with him. My response is that I focused on what was good about Sheldon—in the same way that I have focused on the positive personality traits of all the individuals for whom I have worked. We all have negative characteristics that can make us difficult to work with in certain situations. By focusing on people's admirable personality traits, I am able to appreciate their unique skills and ways of approaching challenges. I saw what was good about Sheldon and came to hold him in high regard, finding his accomplishments and dedication to charitable acts commendable.

INTERNAL CONFLICTS

Marina Bay Sands was successful, but our food and beverage service was overwhelmed and struggling. I decided to bring in Coder from Macao to address the issue.

Coder immediately had a conflict with the food and beverage manager, an employee Sheldon had hired and known for years. Sheldon heard about the conflict and told me to remove Coder. When I ended Coder's contract, I knew that he had money in stock options in the company and would be OK financially. Years later, I learned that during his time at Marina Bay Sands, Coder had made changes that helped the company immensely. Removing Coder was very difficult for me and not an action that I took lightly, but it was Sheldon's call. Coder was one of my best employees, and to this day, I am uncomfortable with the way the relationship between Coder and Marina Bay Sands ended. My consolation is that Coder benefited financially from his LVS experience, and he went on to do great things in Asia.

Jacobs also continued to be a problem. At the Marina Bay Sands opening, Jacobs came to Singapore and confronted Marina Bay Sands CEO Arasi. Jacobs did not approve of certain aspects of the Marina Bay Sands facility. His confrontation was another example of overstepping. As usual, Jacobs did not communicate through the proper channels.

The night of the Marina Bay Sands opening, I went to talk to Sheldon about Jacobs. Sheldon was getting dressed for the black-tie dinner.

"I want to fire Jacobs," I told Sheldon.

"Fine," Sheldon said. Then he reminded me, "I wanted to fire him earlier."

I didn't have a person in mind to replace Jacobs, but I knew that letting Jacobs go was the right decision for the company.

A couple of weeks later, I flew to Macao with board member and head of the Audit Committee Irwin Segal to terminate Jacobs. Segal had volunteered to stay in Macao as interim CEO until Jacobs was replaced permanently. I had already discussed the termination with Sheldon and told him that Jacobs was entitled to his bonus. I had also mentioned to Sheldon that if I terminated Jacobs for cause, he wouldn't get his stock options. My suggestion was that I terminate him without cause so that he could have his stock options. My view was that employees earned their stock options during their terms of employment and therefore should keep their options upon termination. Also, giving employees their stock options did not cost the company very much money. Allowing employees to keep stock options was a matter of terminating them properly and with compassion. Unless there had been theft or something egregious, I felt that employees should be treated well even during termination.

But Sheldon was angry with Jacobs. "No, you can't give him his options," Sheldon said.

In the meeting with Jacobs and Segal, I told Jacobs that I was terminating him. "I'm going to let you have your bonus," I said.

"What about my options?" Jacobs asked.

"I can't give them to you."

"If you don't give me my options, I am going to the United States government and I'm going to report to them that Sheldon has violated the Foreign Corrupt Practices Act. I have proof."

It was an outrageous claim. Sheldon was an incredibly ethical businessman. He never broke or even bent the rules. I knew that he would never violate the Foreign Corrupt Practices Act. However, it didn't exclude another company employee from having done so.

What I knew for certain was that Jacobs was threatening me. It was an attempt at extortion.

"I can't give you your options," I repeated.

I reported to Sheldon that I didn't give Jacobs his options, that I terminated him, and that he had left the LVS premises. It was the end of one story and the beginning of another.

One month later, we received a letter from the Securities and Exchange Commission and the US Department of Justice stating that they were investigating LVS's behavior in Macao for a possible violation of the Foreign Corrupt Practices Act. The letter directed us to hire independent counsel to investigate the situation. We solicited recommendations from three legal firms, which we later found were populated by retired Justice Department or SEC employees. We also hired lawyers to represent LVS. They began their own investigation into the merits of Jacobs's case. It was a long and arduous process of collecting and compiling documents. As the investigation and case dragged on, the related bills mounted.

GIVE ME A DATE

While the drama with the US Department of Justice investigation continued, I returned to work. I left Irwin Segal to run the operation in Macao while we sought a permanent replacement for Jacobs. Rob Goldstein found two people: Ed Tracy, who came from a hotel and gaming background and had run the Trump Hotels, and David Sisk, who was very knowledgeable about casino operations. Together they helped to improve Sands China's operations.

We were also opening the four hotels on the Cotai Strip for which construction had been stopped earlier. They were the Shangri-La and Traders Hotels set to be managed by the Shangri-La Hotel Company, a British company in Hong Kong that operated hotels in Asia. One day I received a call from the president of Shangri-La asking when the Shangri-La and Traders Hotels would open. We had just put the funding together for the project, and I couldn't estimate a date when the hotels would open. He was impatient.

"I can't give you a date," I said. "Call again in a couple of months."

A couple of months later, he called again. "You have to give me a date," he said.

I said, "How many hotels have you opened during your career?"

"About twenty," he said.

I said, "I've opened about two thousand, and I can't give you a date. I don't know why you think that, at this point, I would be able to give you an opening date."

Six months later, he called and told me that the Shangri-La company was pulling out of the deal. It did not seem like a wise business decision. They had a management contract, which meant that they weren't paying for the hotels, and the company would have collected a fee once the hotel opened. It was a good deal for a small company in a competitive market that was becoming increasingly difficult to penetrate. The Shangri-La Hotel Company charged us an $80,000 penalty, which paled in comparison to the money they could have made had they been patient. I sent a check immediately.

In the twenty-four hours after Shangri-La revoked our contract, Chris Nassetta, the CEO of Hilton, called me. I called him back, as well as the president of Holiday Inn, Kirk Kinsell, within forty-eight hours. Two deals were done with only a handshake: one for a six-hundred-room Conrad and the other for a twelve-hundred-room Holiday Inn. This was made possible by the good relationships I had built with people in the industry.

LVS wanted to continue to grow and open new facilities around the world. By 2014, our operations in Singapore, Macao, Bethlehem, Las Vegas, and elsewhere were doing well, and we were looking to open in new locations. Sheldon had always wanted to open a location in Madrid. We planned five resorts in Spain.

Two things happened then. First, Goldstein, along with Sheldon's son-in-law, Patrick Dumont (who had replaced Ken Kay), didn't like the idea of opening resorts in Spain. Then the prime minister of Spain informed LVS that he anticipated trouble getting the deal passed by the EU Competition Committee. LVS facilities in Spain would have brought forty thousand construction jobs and forty thousand permanent employee jobs to the Spanish economy that had a 55 percent youth unemployment rate and a 28 percent general unemployment rate—it would have been great for the country. Through LVS, Sheldon had improved the economies of Las Vegas and Macao, and I believed that he could improve the economy of Spain. There was nothing like the facility we intended to build on the entire European continent. Sheldon could have changed the entire continent. But between Goldstein, Dumont, and the prime minister of Spain, Sheldon was convinced not to go forward with the project. This was the first indicator to me that I was losing my influence at the top of the company.

SHELDON ADELSON

Sheldon has always been politically involved with the governments of both the United States and the State of Israel. Although he is now a prominent Republican, at one time Sheldon was a Democrat. While I worked at LVS, I had long conversations with Sheldon about politics and principles.

In December 2012, Sheldon was in Israel on his annual vacation. He called me and said, "You'll never believe what just happened," he said. "I received a call from President Obama." President Obama was in the process of negotiating with Congress in an effort to avoid sequester.

Sheldon had missed the call, but President Obama was scheduled to call him again the following day.

The next day, I got another call from Sheldon. President Obama's assistant had called and asked, "Is this Mr. Adelson?"

Sheldon said, "Yes."

The next voice on the phone belonged to President Obama. The president said, "Sheldon Adelson, this is President Obama."

"Yes, Mr. President. How are you?" Sheldon said.

"Fine." Then President Obama said to Sheldon, "You are the most important Republican in the United States, and I need your help."

Sheldon said, "Mr. President, I'm an American first and a Republican second. If there is any way I can help you, I will try."

"I need you to help me on the sequester," President Obama said. "I need you to talk to House Majority Leader Eric Cantor and try to convince him to vote to end the sequester."

Sheldon had supported Cantor in the past. "I will try," Sheldon said.

Sheldon got on his plane, flew back to Washington from Israel, and met with Representative Cantor.

Although Sheldon was unable to convince Cantor to vote to end the sequester, he went above and beyond to make a valid effort. Sheldon did everything in his power to help the president of the United States, even though President Obama did not represent the political party that Sheldon supported. The act spoke to Sheldon's values and character. I never forgot it.

THREE CHOICES

In 2014, I had a very good relationship with Sheldon. I had dinner with him and his wife a few nights a week, and we kept in close contact about both professional and personal matters. LVS was doing very well, and there was less demand on me to reorganize and make major changes. I was no longer excited about what I was doing. The job felt done.

"I think there are three things that I can do," I said to Andrea one night. "I can retire at the end of the year, I can continue to work as a consultant and also run Sheldon's foundation, or I can stay in my current position." I couldn't decide if I should stay or go.

In February, I approached David Solomon, our Goldman Sachs representative, with an idea. I thought that we should sell another 20 percent of Sands China stock to a Chinese partner. We were designing a new building in Macao called the Parisian, which would be very successful. If we sold 20 percent to a Chinese partner, LVS would maintain 51 percent of the stock, and the company would basically have a guarantee that the concession would be renewed. Sheldon, who owned 54 percent the company, would get $6 billion, and the shareholders would receive the other $6 billion in cash or dividends.

David Solomon agreed that it was a great idea. Sheldon also liked the idea. Goldstein and Dumont again disagreed with me and turned down the proposal. My ability to create positive change to the status quo was being challenged. The company was doing well anyway and didn't really need me. I decided to retire. I gave Sheldon nine months' notice—enough time to find a replacement. It was March. I would retire in December.

A few weeks after I made the announcement, Rob Goldstein came into my office and said, "I want you to know that if I don't get your job, I'm going to quit."

"Talk to Sheldon," I told him.

Sheldon began looking for my replacement. He interviewed David Solomon from Goldman Sachs for the position. Solomon was only willing to take the position if Sheldon became chairman and gave him the CEO position, which would have allowed him to make all the personnel and compensation decisions. Sheldon declined.

In May 2014, while playing golf on a Saturday afternoon, I received a call from one of the directors, Irwin Chafetz, who was also my very good friend. Chafetz and board member Charlie Foreman needed to speak with me in person. They flew from Boston to Las Vegas the next morning and met me at my golf club.

"There are some problems," they said during the meeting on Sunday. They listed five accusations that had been made against me.

"The first is that you took an airplane that was supposed to go to a customer."

I explained that I had approached someone in the flight department and said that if no one was using the G5, I would like to use it. A customer was using it, and I asked that if the customer canceled, can I be allowed to use the G5?

"The second is that there is a rumor that you are telling people you saved the company."

I had never said that. Sheldon had saved the company by contributing $1 billion of his own money, an act that gave me the time to put a team together and restructure the company.

"The third is that you tried to get someone hired as the assistant director of marketing by threatening the director of marketing with termination if he didn't hire your friend."

It was true that I had told the director of marketing that he needed an assistant and that I had sent someone to interview with him, but I didn't tell the director of marketing that he needed to hire that person, and I never said I would fire anyone for making a good hire.

"The fourth accusation is that you put yourself in front of Sheldon."

They were suggesting that I was assuming authority that was not mine. I said, "When? Where? Never. I've never done that."

"The fifth is that you told T. Rowe Price, one of our largest shareholders, that our stock will go down when you leave the company."

It was preposterous. First, Rob Goldstein was the only person in the company who communicated with T. Rowe Price. Second, I owned seven hundred thousand shares of stock in LVS. Why would I tell anybody that the stock was going down? It made no economic sense.

The accusations themselves made no sense.

"You have to meet with Sheldon tomorrow," Chafetz and Foreman told me.

I went home and spoke to Andrea.

Andrea said, "When you talk to Sheldon, make sure Miriam is in the room. I know Miriam, and she's not going to put up with this."

"Fine," I said, but I was angry that Sheldon was entertaining these accusations. "I think I'm going to quit immediately."

"You have $5 million worth of restricted stock coming to you in December," Andrea said. "You're not going to quit. Just stick it out." Andrea has very good judgment.

I met with Sheldon and Miriam the next day. I went through each of the five accusations categorically and explained why each was false. "Something is wrong here," I said. "I could never have done these things." I was still hurt that Sheldon might believe I was capable of such things. The self-serving and deviant behavior that I was being accused of was out of character for me and went against my core principles.

Sheldon said that he believed me, but things had shifted between us.

Toward the end of my time with LVS, I called the company lawyer and asked who had made the accusations against me. The lawyer wasn't sure. To this day I don't know the identity of my accuser.

MY RETIREMENT PARTY

In December 2014, LVS held a retirement party in my honor. Sheldon gave me a gold watch and made a speech. "Before Mike Leven came to the company, nobody wanted to work here," he said. "After he came to the company, everybody wanted to work here." That was a generous statement by Sheldon, and I really appreciated hearing his feelings.

Miriam told me that if I didn't like the watch, I could trade it in, which I did. A couple of months later, while I was still on the board, I got a 1099 tax form for the watch. I owed $24,000 in tax for the gifts that I received, which I believe Sheldon knew nothing about.

I still don't know why Sheldon Adelson made me president of his company in the first place, but I have a strong feeling that Chafetz recommended me, and Sheldon trusted him. Throughout my career, many opportunities that I was given were based on relationships and building trust and a reputation within the business.

Bernie Marcus was right: Sheldon's net worth went up dramatically while I was CEO of his company. The United States of America and the State of Israel benefited from his success and mine. I did well enough to give away nearly 30 percent of my net worth to charitable endeavors since my retirement. I sincerely regret the loss of friendship with Sheldon Adelson and his family. After fifty-three years of working for various companies and bosses, my departure from LVS was the only one after which my relationship with my boss was not what I expected.

Lessons Learned

75. Do not concentrate on the negative aspects of people's personalities and behaviors; instead, focus on their positive characteristics. Find the good in everyone.

76. When working to turn around a company or a department, you must have people working with you who either have experience turning a company around or who are very quick studies. Some of the people whom you choose to help with the turnaround can be long-term employees of the company, and some must be brought in from outside the company.

77. When taking a new position, it is always good to have colleagues and coworkers in place whom you trust—either people who already work for your new employer or people who you worked with previously and can hire into positions at your new place of work.

78. Sometimes people do not seize great opportunities because they are not comfortable or feel uncertain about their situations. When they are comfortable, they often do not seize great opportunities because change could be dangerous to the future or current comfortable situation.

79. When leaving a job, don't look back. When you know that it is time for you to leave a position, leave as soon as possible.

CONCLUSION

TANK AND THE GEORGIA AQUARIUM

When I retired from LVS in 2014, I had already begun building a house in Boca Raton, Florida, to honor my commitment to Bernie Marcus to move to Saint Andrews upon my retirement. In November 2014, before I officially retired, I received a call from Rick Slagle, a financial adviser for the Marcus Foundation and fellow board member at the Georgia Aquarium. He told me about existing issues with the management of the Georgia Aquarium—among other things, the current CEO was not leading the company, and the company was floundering. Slagle wanted to know if I would consider returning to the aquarium to restructure the management.

I called Bernie. He had been at least partly responsible for me taking the opportunity with the LVS Corporation. If he needed help, I wanted to help him. But I was concerned because, frankly, I didn't want to have a boss again. The years I had spent working under Sheldon were rewarding in many ways, but I was tired of reporting to someone else. Bernie was the chairman of the Georgia Aquarium—I would be reporting to him. I asked the advice of a friend. He suggested that I ask Bernie if he would step into a position of chairman emeritus and allow me to be CEO and chairman of the Georgia Aquarium so that I could seamlessly manage both the operations and the business.

I made the proposal to Bernie. "You could still control the board," I said. "And I would advise you of anything large before doing it, but I want complete control over the operation, the people, and the management."

Bernie agreed.

I told him that I didn't want to be paid: no salary and no bonus. "I'll be the volunteer chairman," I told him. It was about a half-million-dollar donation annually to the Georgia Aquarium.

Bernie told me that I needed to remove the current CEO.

"No," I said. "If you don't want the current CEO there, you tell him he's gone now."

"Who's going to run it between now and when you start?" Bernie asked.

"The current CEO is not really running it now," I said. "Another month won't make a difference."

On January 1, 2015, I took on the last position that I would hold during my career: volunteer CEO and chairman of the Georgia Aquarium.

When I arrived at the Georgia Aquarium, attendance was down. The organization was frozen, having not instituted new ideas in the past several years. Because the previous CEO had not been actively leading the company, it was being run by the Financial Audit Committee of the board—a body designed and prepared to advise, not to run, a company. Employees and the people managing the departments—the people closest to the product and customers—were not allowed to make decisions. Employees and management were showing up and doing their respective work, but nobody was thinking about the future. I needed them to think creatively. On the positive side, the Georgia

Aquarium had access to cash flow, but they were not spending their money effectively.

The aquarium was in the process of building a turtle exhibit. I asked the staff why they had chosen to build a turtle exhibit. No one could give me an answer. It wasn't a good sign.

"Whose idea was it?" I asked.

No one knew. It seemed that the idea had been externally generated.

I asked a third question. "Is the turtle exhibit going to expand attendance? Is it going to excite visitors so that they either come to the aquarium for the first time or come back? Is it worthwhile from a marketing perspective?"

The immediate answer from everyone was no. It would be an exhibit that visitors would enjoy, but it was not a dynamic exhibit.

"What exhibit would excite visitors?" I asked.

"Sea lions." Everyone agreed.

I told Bernie and the board that rather than build a turtle exhibit, we were going to build a sea lion exhibit. We had spent about $6 million in construction on the turtle exhibit that we would lose, but I was convinced that the change would recover the loss in the end.

The near-mistake of building a new turtle exhibit rather than something that would bring visitors to the aquarium was evidence of a larger issue at the Georgia Aquarium: a lack of communication. The people in various departments at the aquarium did not talk to one another. The aquarium was completely siloed. I needed to get them to work as a team.

As a team, one of the first issues that we needed to deal with was related to potential problems that could arise as a result of not building the new turtle exhibit. I knew of one such issue from my previous time at the aquarium: canceling the new exhibit would displace a

550-pound turtle named Tank who had been rescued and housed by the aquarium for years. "What will happen to Tank?" I asked the administrative staff.

They planned to send him back to the institution in Florida from where he'd come. I didn't like the idea.

"Can he go into the Georgia Explorer Exhibit?" I asked. The Georgia Explorer Exhibit was a huge, six-million-gallon exhibit that held whale sharks, manta rays, other small sharks, and groupers.

Moving Tank into the Georgia Explorer Exhibit seemed plausible from an administrative perspective, so I talked to the people in the marine department, but they had concerns about putting Tank in the Explorer Exhibit. "He bites," they said.

The Georgia Explorer Exhibit offered profitable guided scuba dives and snorkeling for visitors. Employees in the marine department were concerned that Tank might bite a visitor on a dive.

"Visitors go into the exhibit with a guide," I pointed out, "and the guide has a stick to keep the groupers and other animals away from the visitors. Can't the guide also keep Tank away?"

That made sense. The marine department agreed to allow Tank into the exhibit, and Tank has been extremely happy there ever since. The culture between departments was beginning to change and lines of communication were opening.

The aquarium was also trying to acquire beluga whales. They had purchased and were paying to care for beluga whales in Russia, but the National Oceanic and Atmospheric Administration, the federal agency responsible for the oversight of fisheries, had prevented the whales from entering the US. The Georgia Aquarium was enmeshed in an ongoing lawsuit with the federal government over the issue. It was costing the aquarium money both in legal costs and in costs of caring for the animals overseas. I dropped the lawsuit and sold the Russian whales to certified aquariums in Asia.

Next, I reviewed the marketing and public relations operations at the aquarium. The current marketing campaign was not doing well. Consequently, the aquarium's attendance was low. In addition, there were management problems with the food operations—the catering, which was outsourced to the Wolfgang Puck Company, had priced us out of our main market and caused our banqueting sales to decrease. No one was paying attention to the customers and what they wanted.

I brought in a new senior director of marketing named Martin Gray whom I knew from the hospitality business. I brought in Debbie Campbell, with whom I had worked at US Franchise Systems, to be Gray's assistant. I moved some of the existing marketing department employees into positions that better suited their skills. Then we had a good team and good leadership in place in the marketing department.

It took a little less than a year to build the sea lion exhibit, and in the next four years, the marketing department continued to improve, as did the Georgia Aquarium's internal communications. Within five years cash flow increased to $41 million providing enough capital so that we by then owned (rather than leased) all our animals. The operating margin went from 22 percent to 41 percent, and the attendance went from about 1.8 million to 2.5 million visitors annually. The aquarium is currently building a $130 million expansion that will include a shark exhibit that will be the only one of its kind in North America. They are also adding a new restaurant to help meet the demands of the growing food and banquet business. Animal Planet has done two major series on the Georgia Aquarium. The Georgia Aquarium is a model of how you can make a nonprofit organization generate earnings for expansion and continue to meet the needs of a community for purposes of education, entertainment, and tourist attraction that brings business to the city.

After five years, the Georgia Aquarium was doing well and it was time to leave. I retired for the third and last time. The CEO and the CFO who replaced me both have incredible experience and knowledge and are well suited to their positions.

When I announced my retirement, I received several letters from the board and other people involved with the aquarium. One was from board member and Treasurer Jim Grien.

October 21, 2019

Dear Mike,

I read your announcement last week with mixed emotions. On the other hand, it was reason for me to smile and reflect, something I do too infrequently, on your tender [sic] as our CEO and all you've done to guide the Georgia Aquarium to the profoundly positive place we find ourselves.

Conversely, it marks from me, the end of the collaboration with you that I cherish, both professionally and personally. You are an extraordinary leader. Your insight is one always on the mark. Your marketing feel and creative vision are extraordinary. Your ability to engender loyalty from a team of empowered senior executives is rare. And you're [sic] skill as a communicator never ceases to amaze me. Most of all, you personify the power of lifelong learning. I am forever amazed by the breadth of what you know.

I am looking forward to the December 3rd celebration, your going away party, and what I'm sure will be future opportunities to work with you and learn from you. Most importantly, I love you as a friend and mentor. Thanks for all you've done for this organization and for me.

Sincerely,

Jim Grien

What I learned during my long career before I became the volunteer CEO of the Georgia Aquarium was that after all is said and done, a leader and boss is only as successful as their employees. When you understand that fact, you can make any company or organization a success. People are at the core of any company, and therefore communicating with and listening to people is vital. It is the human side of any industry that matters.

> **It is the human side of any industry that matters.**

No leader is successful alone. Even those who are in charge of an organization or situation are part of a system that includes people who play, people who work, and people who live; people who have personalities, personal concerns, and ideas about how things can or should happen. If, as a leader or as a person in power, you can concentrate your efforts on ensuring that you give those people opportunities, they will make your company or organization a success.

In Jim Grien's letter, he said that I had "empowered" others. That is a critical component of success. As a leader, I learned that individual people were most successful when I gave them personal freedom to create their work and the opportunity, tools, and support they needed to complete tasks in collaboration with others. If a leader does this for their employees, nothing can stop the organization from being successful. It never ceases to amaze me how well people work when given the opportunity to do so.

During my career, I learned from every boss I had, from the

very beginning until the very end. At the end of my career, I was able to apply all that I had learned and to see the success of those years of learning.

MICHAEL AND ANDREA LEVEN FAMILY FOUNDATION

I continue to sit on the board of the Georgia Aquarium, as well as other boards, but my efforts now are focused on giving charitably. For me, philanthropy is the reward and result of a successful business career.

When I retired from LVS, I started a small foundation with $25 million, which I manage along with two directors: my eldest son, Jon Leven, and my wife, Andrea. The foundation gives money to a variety of causes that are important to me—many that are nontraditional. I prefer to support small projects where my foundation can make a big impact with $50,000 or $100,000 donations. I have financed several start-ups and small organizations. I also fund educational opportunities for underrepresented populations and first-generation college students. I am still guided by the values and principles that I developed as a young person toward inclusion and against discrimination.

I also give back to the organizations and institutions that helped to make me a success, including Boston Latin School, where I went to high school; Tufts University, where I went to college; Boston University, where I went to graduate school; a leadership conference for the Alpha Epsilon Pi fraternity; a leadership conference at the Hotel Marketing Association; and Jewish organizations such as Birthright Israel. My sons also encouraged me to fund a hospitality school at Kennesaw State University in Georgia from my personal funds. I now have an endowed professorship at Kennesaw State in the Leven School of Management, Entrepreneurship, and Hospitality, which resides in the College of Business. I am a big fan of Kennesaw State University, which is a public institution that hosts many first-generation students.

My recent project is called the Jewish Future Pledge, an organization that works with people who are leaving charitable resources in either wills or trusts. Participants pledge to leave 50 percent or more of their charitable resources to Jewish causes and the State of Israel and the other 50 percent to other causes of import to them. The Jewish Future Pledge is especially dear to me. The cost of supporting Jewish causes and the State of Israel continues to increase; if donations do not also increase, those causes will fail. It is important to me that Jewish traditions and values are passed on, as they were passed on from my grandparents and my parents to me.

The intent of the Michael and Andrea Leven Family Foundation is to make contributions that exhaust the funds during my lifetime. Over the last five and a half years, I have spent the initial amount down to $1.5 million. I learned from working with the Marcus Foundation that passing on a foundation to the next generation is very difficult. Bernie's foundation will outlive him, and because of this, he was advised by a consultant to draft purposes, objectives, and structures that could direct the inheritors of his foundation on how to spend the foundation's money. This process seemed like one that would be complicated both for me and for those left to manage my foundation. I want my legacy to be the contributions made by my foundation and the ways that these contributions improve the lives of others—something I will have the privilege of knowing during my lifetime—rather than the foundation itself. Mostly, I don't need my foundation—and my name—to be around after I am gone. Rather than talking about me in decades to come, I hope that people will be talking about my children and my children's children and all the wonderful ways they are having a positive effect on the world. My ideal legacy is having empowered others to do good and to be successful.

APPENDIX

WHY BUSINESSES LOSE CUSTOMERS

Serving the organization instead of your customers is foolish. Ignoring your customers is wrong. Failing to listen and respond to them is deadly. Don't become internally focused. Keep your sights set on the maintenance and acquisition of customers.

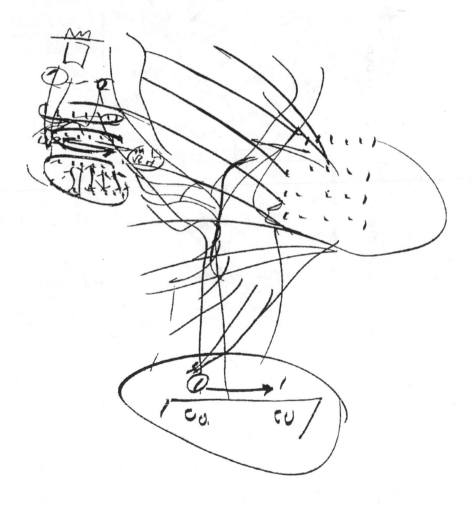

THE VISION EXPLAINED (START AT THE BOTTOM.)

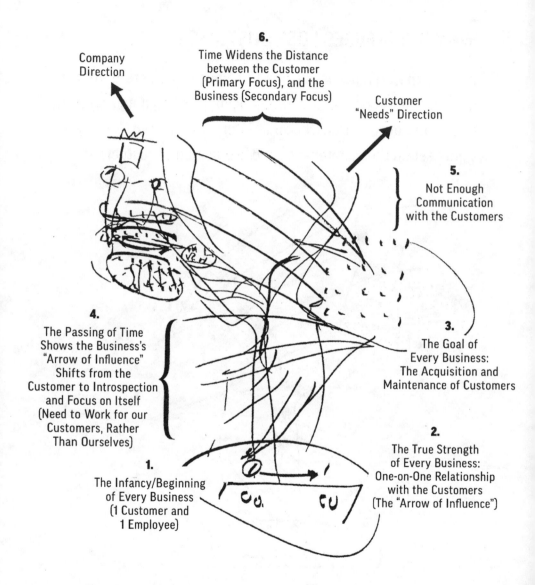

6.
Time Widens the Distance between the Customer (Primary Focus), and the Business (Secondary Focus)

Company Direction

Customer "Needs" Direction

5.
Not Enough Communication with the Customers

4.
The Passing of Time Shows the Business's "Arrow of Influence" Shifts from the Customer to Introspection and Focus on Itself (Need to Work for our Customers, Rather Than Ourselves)

3.
The Goal of Every Business: The Acquisition and Maintenance of Customers

2.
The True Strength of Every Business: One-on-One Relationship with the Customers (The "Arrow of Influence")

1.
The Infancy/Beginning of Every Business (1 Customer and 1 Employee)

Mike's father, David Leven

Mike's mother, Sari Leven

Mike's wife, Andrea Leven

Andrea's parents, Selma and Charlie Aronson

Pa Frank Goldberg and Mike, 1941

NOVEMBER 1948

Thanksgiving, 1948

Jon Leven (son) and family

Adam Leven (son) and family

Rob Leven (son) and family

Mike and family